The Coazze Notebook

Luigi Pirandello

Translation and Introduction
by Lisa Sarti

BORDIGHERA PRESS
NEW YORK, NEW YORK

Robert Viscusi Essay Series
Volume 5

This book series is dedicated to the long essay. It intends to publish those studies that are longer than the traditional journal-length essay and yet shorter than the traditional book-length manuscript.

Lisa Sarti and Bordighera Press thank Dr. Rosario Maniscalco for facilitating the publication of *The Coazze Notebook* as well as for permission to include the images listed below. A special thanks to Houghton Library at Harvard University for letting us publish the missing page of the Notebook

Parco Archeologico e Paesaggistico della Valle dei Templi di Agrigento – Biblioteca – Museo "Luigi Pirandello" di Agrigento

1. Coazze Bell Tower (Campanile di Coazze)
2. Medieval Building (Edificio medievale)
3. Lamp and Candle (Lampada e candela)
4. Head Portrait (Testa d'uomo)
5. Clown (Pagliaccio)

ISBN 978-1-59954-154-9
Library of Congress Control Number: 202194510

BORDIGHERA PRESS
John D. Calandra Italian American Institute
25 West 43rd Street, 17th Floor
New York, NY 10038

To my beloved mamma,

who left too soon to see this book in print.

Table of Contents

Acknowledgements (vii)

Preface, by Dr. Rosario Maniscalco
and Dr. Roberto Sciarratta (x)

Introduction (1)

- Italian Editions and the First English Translation. (4)
- Geography and *The Coazze Notebook* (9)
- *The Coazze Notebook* as Source Text (13)
- Visual Art in *The Coazze Notebook* (16)
- Language in *The Coazze Notebook* (19)
- Introducing *The Coazze Notebook* to Anglophone Readers (23)

The Coazze Notebook (27)

List of Books (59)

The Missing Page (61)

Bibliography (69)

Index of Names and Works (73)

About the Author (81)

About the Editor (85)

Acknowledgments

The idea for this project was born at the same time that the pandemic forced the world into domestic confinement. As I sheltered in place, I found solace in Pirandello's *Coazze Notebook*. As I ventured on solitary walks around my urban neighborhood, I began to think of his walks along tranquil Alpine trails, all meticulously recorded in his notebook. Indeed, I was inspired. I delighted in the playwright's moments of ecstatic contemplation and inner peace. I could picture him on his train ride from Rome to the Alps or see him gazing at the iconic church at the entrance of the charming hamlet of Coazze, while greeting and interacting with the locals whom he sketched so vividly in his notes.

Translating Pirandello's notes left me with the same deep impressions that the landscape and colorful idioms left on him. It also prompted a look back at my own Tuscan upbringing, which came in handy when rendering the vernacular expressions Pirandello jotted down into English. The wonder he experienced at the colorful sayings he heard is the same wonder my friends from other regions of Italy experienced when I tested my thoughts for this translation on them. These tests triggered much laughter and hilarious conversation, but also reminded me of Italy's vernacular richness: you can pair two Italians from different regions of the country, and they would be unintelligible to one another.

Although this project was a somewhat solitary adventure, it would not have come into being without the help, encouragement, and generous support of many people, even those who just listened to my brainstorming. To the elderly speakers of local Tuscan dialects, I owe the greatest debt—without their lived experience, my early childhood memories of quaint proverbs and vernacular expressions (which I heard so often) might have faded and become unusable. Other than enabling me to translate Pirandello's notes, their help allowed me to enter into conversation, simultaneously, with Pirandello himself and with my ancestors.

My family and friends played a significant role in this project, offering invaluable advice and enthusiastic support—it's hard not to thank everyone by name. The same could be said for the colleagues with whom I shared thoughts about this translation, including Paolo Fasoli, Pietro Frassica, Carlo Di Lieto, Maria Enrico, Patrizia Comello Perry, Michael Subialka, Stefano Boselli, and Christopher Lapinski. Let me then express my gratitude to *all* who contributed to this project with their competence in languages and Italian literature, their encouragement and praise, their cheerful conversation, and their good sense of humor. You all know what your support has meant to me. A special thanks goes out to my sister Elisabetta and my brother-in-law Ezio for their resilience in negotiating our different time zones and for always interspersing our conversations with a good dose of Florentine jargon.

The Coazze Notebook was translated not just to introduce the English-speaking reader to local expressions and breathtaking landscapes in the Piedmont, but to present Pirandello at the very beginning of his artistic career. His notes from this period, differing in tone and style from his later fictional works, reveal an author in search of fame, subject matter, his own voice, and freedom from inner torment. I am grateful to CUNY's Professional Staff Congress (Grant B–Cycle 50) for financing my archival research and awarding me the opportunity to tread the same paths as Pirandello and to visit the places that would become the setting of many of his narratives.

To the staff at the Biblioteca Museo Regionale Luigi Pirandello in Agrigento, which went the extra mile to ensure I had the resources to carry out this project, I am deeply grateful. Cristina Angela Iacono, in particular, provided invaluable archival support and fellowship. I also wish to thank Dr. Rosario Maniscalco and Dr. Roberto Sciarratta for granting me permission to include Pirandello's drawings, which have enriched this publication.

Thanks to everyone on the Bordighera Press team for providing skillful help with the logistics of assembling the material and crafting the book's interior and jacket. I am particularly grateful to its co-director, Professor Anthony Julian Tamburri, for his enthusiasm and assistance throughout the publication process. Finally, I must acknowledge the tremendous help and support I received from the staff of the Houghton Library at Harvard University, and especially from Professor Ombretta Frau of Mount Holyoke College, in retrieving the notebook's missing page.

If it is true that a book always finds its way to readers, then I hope this one will find its way to my beloved late parents. Thanks to them, I developed an intimate awareness and appreciation for the richness of the Italian language and culture. In hindsight, my multicultural upbringing proved to be a greater asset than my bilingualism in carrying out this translation project, and for that I'd like to dedicate this book to my *mamma*. She and I had many illuminating conversations on the idioms in Coazze and Montepulciano during her last days.

A final thanks goes to my husband Andrea and our daughter Chiara for their untiring enthusiasm in welcoming and supporting me through another Pirandello project!

Preface

The main objectives of a library include not only the recovery and acquisition of bibliographic and documentary material, but also, and above all, the study of the collections kept there. The aim must be to create editions of works and catalogs that will be valuable tools of investigation for the scholarly community as well as for cultural promotion to the public. In this perspective of exposure, between 1994 and 2002, the Luigi Pirandello Regional Library Museum of Agrigento, today the technical-scientific structure of the Archaeological Park Valley of the Temples of Agrigento, took advantage of the funds made available by the Sicilian Region to acquire the Archive "Eredi Stefano Pirandello."

Impressive and of great historical, artistic, and literary value, the archives proved to be fundamenttal to understanding the human and psychological events of Luigi Pirandello, which, as we know, are intimately connected to that which inspired his art. The vast and precious collection of documentary material has made it possible to preserve not only manuscripts, typescripts, and press drafts of published works, but also fragments and notes of works that were never brought to fruition, memorabilia, unpublished writings, theatrical scripts, autographed documents, a substantial epistolary, newspaper clippings, magazines and photographs, and—last but not least—the three precious handwritten notebooks: the *Taccuino di Bonn,* the *Taccuino di Coazze* and the *Taccuino Provenzale.*

In 1998, for the project of the then director Giuseppe Lo Iacono, and with the collaboration of Calogero Camilleri, Filomena Capobianco, and Cristina Angela Iacono, the Luigi Pirandello Library Museum, in continuing the initiatives commendably started, published the *Taccuino di Coazze* in a facsimile reproduction with transcription of the facing text.[1] From this publication today comes the critical edition in English, edited by Professor Lisa Sarti, Professor of Italian Studies at the City University of New York, which has added a further step to the dissemination of Pirandello's *Taccuino*, making it accessible to an English-speaking and hence greater international audience. Besides helping to overcome language barriers, the English edition is added to the publications edited by the Library of Agrigento and constitutes an important step in the overall scientific project of publishing the bibliographic patrimony of manuscripts preserved. In fact, the English edition publishes for the first time the paper manuscript (recto and verso) missing from the *Taccuino*, found only in 2001 in the archives of the Houghton Library of Harvard University,[2] as well as the drawings omitted from the Mondadori edition of the *Taccuino di Coazze* edited by Manlio Lo Vecchio Musti.

We would therefore like to express our gratitude to Professor Lisa Sarti for her dedication and thoroughness, and we extend our thanks to Professor Anthony Julian Tamburri in his capacity as Co-director of Bordighera Press in New York. To this publication goes the merit of promoting, at an international level, the program of valorization and dissemination of the documentary patrimony of Luigi Pirandello held in the Library Museum of Agrigento.

A special thanks to Cristina Angela Iacono, head of the Historical Fund of the Library, who with generosity and competence, has facilitated the definition of the project in

---

[1] Luigi Pirandello, *Taccuino di Coazze*, autograph manuscript with sketch of the bell tower of the Mother Church of Coazze (To), cart.; 1901 - 1910. Agrigento, Parco Archeologico e Paesaggistico della Valle dei Templi-Biblioteca Museo Luigi Pirandello di Agrigento, Archivio Eredi Stefano Pirandello, inv. 5989.

[2] The missing paper, accompanied by its transcription, has been included in the volume *Pirandello e il Piemonte: atti del Convegno internazionale di studi 16-17 novembre 2001* (Turin: Edizioni Enterprise GFS Communication, 2004) 36-37, which also includes the critical essay by Ombretta Frau, "La tessera mancante del *Taccuino di Coazze*," ibid., 38-44.

order to promote and disseminate a wider knowledge of the *Taccuino di Coazze.*

We hope that this will be the beginning of a fruitful and future international collaboration, which will bring Pirandello's work to the universal recognition it deserves.

Roberto Sciarratta
Director of Archaeological and Landscape Park of the Valley of the Temples of Agrigento

Rosario Maniscalco
Director U.O. 5 - Luigi Pirandello Library Museum

INTRODUCTION

According to his notes, Luigi Pirandello arrived in Coazze, a small hamlet in the Piedmont in northern Italy, at 10:46 pm on August 22nd, 1901.[1] He was accompanied by his wife Maria Antonietta Portulano and their three children. They came by train from Rome, where they had been living in financial straits. Although the future Nobel laureate had by then published his first novel, *L'esclusa* (*The Outcast*), along with two collections of poems, several remarkable essays, and a number of well-received short stories, it would be years before he gained worldwide recognition. Nevertheless, for an author in search of inspiration and a creative refuge, the trip was a salutary one. The Pirandellos stayed with Luigi's beloved sister Lina, who wintered in Turin and spent her summers in the Alps. The days were spent eating hearty food, strolling in the woods, and taking in the stunning scenery. Pirandello fell in love with Coazze, staying there until October 11th, far longer than expected.[2] In

---

1 The date and time of Pirandello's arrival in Coazze are reported in a telegram the playwright sent from Rome to his brother-in-law Calogero De Castro. The telegram is part of Renata Marsili Antonetti's personal collection and was included in the transcription of the original *Coazze Notebook* curated by Filomena Capobianco for the Biblioteca-Museo Luigi Pirandello in Agrigento, Italy. The original *Notebook* was part of the personal archive of Stefano Pirandello's heirs, which was acquired by Sicily's Regional Administration in 1994 to be made available to scholars and the public.

2 The date of Pirandello's departure from Coazze is confirmed by a page on Lina's calendar, with a penciled note: "Luigi left for Rome with Antonietta and the kids after spending a month and a half together with us in Coazze." This document is also part of Antonetti's personal collection and included in Capobianco's edition.

his recollections, he would describe the experience as "unforgettable."[3]

During his sojourn, the Maestro kept a notebook in which he recorded everything that caught his eye, from the natives' peculiar manners and dialect to the fast-changing scenery on his walks along picturesque trails. These notes and impressions gave way to poems, illustrations, and storylines, all merging into a seemingly experimental text encompassing graphic art, fiction, and autobiography. The *Coazze Notebook,* as it came to be known, is a compendium of literary criticism, illuminating and emotionally charged personal reflections, vernacular expressions, and sharply observed geographical descriptions. The notes are fragmentary, and occasionally embellished, but they shed light on Pirandello's mode of thought and, in particular, how the ideas he gathered from real life were incorporated into his writing.

The original manuscript consists of twenty-seven pages, eighteen of which are blank and three that were missing until 2001, when one of the torn-out pages, written recto and verso, was found in the archives of Houghton Library at Harvard University. The missing page is now included in this English translation. The handwritten notes in the notebook are interspersed with a total of six drawings in the following order: a sketch of the local bell tower with the sign "Each in His Own Way" (i.e., the inspiration for the 1924 play), an outline of a medieval building, a drawing of a candle and a lamp, a portrait sketch, and a drawing of a miniature jester. Together these illustrations form a visual narrative, capturing not only

---

[3] From a letter Pirandello wrote to his sister, dated December 22, 1901. The letter is part of Antonetti's private collection and is included in the transcription of the *Coazze Notebook*, ed. Capobianco.

Pirandello's experiences but also his habit of thinking visually. The drawings are undated, making it difficult to situate them in time or place, and they appear to have little, if any, intentional design. The remaining eighteen blank pages suggest that Pirandello must have, at some point, stopped using his notepad to jot down his thoughts.

Measuring approximately 5 in. x 3.5 in., the notebook is smaller than a Moleskine, thus more portable but also limited in how much one can write. Pirandello found ways to negotiate these size constraints, as seen on the very last page where a couplet (evoking Coazze's Alpine views and snowy winters) and the beginning of a recipe are written upside-down. It is unclear why the writings are upside-down and separated from the other notes, but their layout does reveal Pirandello's unpremeditated use of his notepad. The notes also show that he alternated between pencil and pen to record his thoughts and make his sketches, using whatever writing instrument was available to him in the moment. This eccentric style suggests not just the spontaneity of Pirandello's reflections, but also the urgency to record what he saw and heard, as if he was afraid of losing his momentum.

The end of the notebook looks like a haphazard ledger, showing expenses and earnings marked down in scattered calculations, along with four lists detailing literary projects (essays, reviews, translations) and academic assignments for which Pirandello was compensated in 1909, 1910, 1905 and 1904. His incomes are not recorded in chronological order, and in some years, they are only partially annotated—emblematic of the unsystematic character of some of the notebook's pages. Nevertheless, these financial records are useful in charting the trajectory of Pirandello's career. They show his rise from a penniless artist with big literary aspirations—feverishly contributing short stories to journals and magazines—to his arrival as an accomplished author, sought out by the most prestigious publishers of his time. In these early years, we see Pirandello make his theatrical debut, consolidate his theory of humor, and find international acclaim with the publication of his iconic novel, *The Late Mattia Pascal* (1904).

In addition to the financial records, the *Notebook*'s final section contains a second set of notes (on two sheets), taken not in Coazze, but in Montepulciano, a small village in the Tuscan countryside between Florence and Siena. Pirandello stayed there briefly in the summer of 1903 following his appointment as examiner at a local school. These writings are commonly referred to by scholars as the *Montelpulciano Notes,* as distinct from the Coazze notes. Although short, they exhibit Pirandello's deep interest in local languages and their influence on standard Italian. Indeed, the *Montelpuciano Notes* are rife with colorful Tuscan idioms and expressions used by the locals, which the playwright meticulously documented out of both curiosity and a sense of amusement. These notes are as invaluable a display of Pirandello's *modus scribendi* as are the Coazze notes. Like the latter, they would be systematically re-used in the author's narrative patterns and plotlines, shaping the dialogue in his plays and other creative works.

Italian Editions and the First English Translation

Several editions of the *Coazze Notebook* have been published over the years, not all of them faithful to the manuscript's original content. The first printed text appeared during Pirandello's lifetime, in 1934, and was curated by Italian writer and film director Lucio D'Ambra, and published (abridged) in the literary journal *Nuova Antologia,* to which Pirandello himself was a prolific contributor. Other publications followed: one in 1938, as part of the *Almanacco Letterario Bompiani,* and another in 1952, in the theater journal *Sipario,* prefaced by an essay written by Pirandello's close friend, Corrado Alvaro. The text as we know it today finally appeared in 1960 as a reference volume, curated by Manlio Lo Vecchio-Musti for the comprehensive Mondadori series. This edition, to the dismay of Pirandello scholars, dispensed with the notebook's visual content and the accounting figures (except for incomes Pirandello reported for the year 1904).

The absence of Pirandello's drawings from some of these publications, especially the Mondadori edition, was likely the catalyst for a new volume published in 2000. This was preceded by an unabridged version that appeared in 1998, which was revised and updated through funding by the Biblioteca-Museo of Luigi Pirandello in Agrigento. This expanded edition contained an appendix with archival findings and documents linked to the *Notebook,* including a copy of a handwritten page, a complete bibliography of the literary and critical works owned or alluded to by Pirandello, and pictures of contemporary Coazze and its landmarks. Moreover, it cited the three missing pages from the manuscript, two of which would be found in the Harvard archive only two years later.

It is also worth mentioning that the 2000 edition curated by Filomena Capobianco preserves Pirandello's fluctuating use of pen and pencil with a typescript that alternates between black and gray ink. Not only are the notes in their original order, but so are the nonchronological list of incomes, the scattered calculations, and the arrangement of the illustrations. The only oddity that was regularized was the upside-down orientation of the closing notes (i.e., the recipe and the couplet), here turned right-side up to facilitate readability.

Using the 1960 Mondadori edition and the 2000 Agrigento publication as its main source texts, this English-language edition diverges from previous ones in certain ways.[4] Most importantly, the six illustrations in the original manuscript were restored and arranged in their original place and order. The motive behind this decision was twofold: first, to remind readers of the *Notebook*'s immense interest as both a textual and visual artifact, and secondly, to show the influence of visuality on Pirandello as a writer, philosopher, and painter. Recent scholarship on the role of imagery in Pirandello's work is beginning to shed light on his life as a painter, which has largely been overshadowed by his son Fausto's artistic career. Numerous articles cited in the bibliography (added only in this English edition) address the subject of Pirandello's visual thought and writing style.

The Mondadori edition served as a reference for the order in which a couplet celebrating the beauty of Coazze appeared. In the manuscript, it is found in the final pages of the manuscript, inverted; here, the couplet is left in the same position as in the Mondadori edition: at the end of the notes taken in Coazze and right before those jotted down in Montepulciano.

---

[4] Luigi Pirandello, *Il taccuino di Coazze*, in *Saggi, Poesie e Scritti varii*, edited by Manlio Lo Vecchio-Musti (Milan: Mondadori, 1960) 1237-1246.

Keeping it here helped sustain continuity and foster readability. As for the list of books Pirandello wrote down right before recording his yearly incomes (the list does not appear in the Mondadori edition), this new edition includes the list at the very end of the notes, together with a facsimile of the page found in the Harvard archive.

Another distinguishing feature of this edition is the inclusion of Pirandello's finances as they appear in the 2000 version, leaving out only a short list of expenses related to everyday items (cigarettes, coffee, newspapers, etc.). Though seemingly irrelevant, these tabulations acquaint the reader with the pragmatic side of the Maestro's concerns, while also demonstrating the scope of his literary achievements and collaborations. For instance, the 1902 report provides the English-language reader with information about Pirandello's close connection to the Genoese literary journal *La Riviera Ligure*, a partnership that lasted almost a decade (1900–1909), with the years 1900 to 1905 being the most productive. Around the same time, Pirandello fell into financial difficulties. In 1903, the year he was appointed exam commissioner in Tuscany, his family's sulfur mine was destroyed in a flood. The loss of this main source of income was devastating for Antonietta, who gradually succumbed to mental illness and was permanently hospitalized in a mental asylum in 1918. More than ever, Pirandello was desperate to capitalize on his writing, selling his works to journals and magazines, even those he had previously submitted royalty-free.

Unlike the Mondadori, this edition includes Pirandello's 1909 and 1910 statements (in the notebook, these dates are reversed) in order to show the flowering of his literary career in the years after Coazze. The year 1909 was a particularly prosperous one. In addition to a short story ("Due letti a due" – "Two Double Beds"), a poem ("Tra castagni e olivi" – "Among Chestnut and Olive Trees"), and several reviews ("Sul Bosforo d'Italia" – "On the Italian Bosphorus" and "La camminante" – "The Walker"), Pirandello published one of his major critical essays, "Teatro siciliano?" ("Sicilian Theater?"), which explored the question of whether Italian dialect could give birth to a thriving regional theater in Italy. In 1910, his novel *The Late Mattia Pascal* received a second printing, just a few years after its German and French publication had won him international fame. (The expenses for foreign translators are among those reported in the *Notebook*.) In that same year, Pirandello debuted his one-act play *La morsa* (*The Vise*), which launched his career as a playwright.

While staking his claim to Italian theater, Pirandello became a staunch advocate of Sicilian-dialect productions, insisting they should be staged on the Italian mainland. We see this borne out in his collaborations with actor Angelo Musco and dramatist Nino Martoglio, as well as in his plays of those years (e.g., *Sicilian Limes, Cecè, Think it Over, Giacomino!, Liolà*), which are redolent of *verismo*. Convinced that the vernacular was a livelier form of expression and realism than standard Italian, Pirandello even wrote some of these plays in Sicilian.

Although he later moved away from regional theater, Pirandello never stopped searching for the perfect literary language, one that could vividly illustrate cultural difference. He found inspiration in local vernacular, especially in the Coazze dialect, and incorporated folksy proverbs, idioms, and adages into his fiction. From an early age, he was aware not just of the role that culture plays in shaping behaviors and traditions, but also of the dialogism between standard language and its dialects, a phenomenon he began exploring in his 1891 dissertation on the Girgenti dialect. The subject recurs throughout his critical and artistic work.

GEOGRAPHY AND THE *COAZZE NOTEBOOK*

Throughout the *Notebook*, Pirandello's fondness for Coazze's local geography grows as he becomes more acquainted with it. In these pages, the Sangone Valley—nestled between the charming crags of Val di Susa and Val Chisone, two of the most famous valleys in the Cottian Alps—is revealed to us impressionistically. We learn about Coazze's residential area, a vast and sunny plateau formed by clay deposits and glacial sediments, delimited by the Sangone River in the south and the Alpine massif of Rocciavré to the west.

The most striking element of these descriptions, however, is the interlacing pattern of feeling and observation. The imagery is so vivid, one can easily picture the wet meadows and chestnut trees in the lower Alps, the wide grazing lands dotted with conifers and rhododendrons, the majestic snowy summits overhead sheltering the valley from colder winds, the small lakes at the foot of the mountains, and the waterfalls reverberating in Coazze's alleyways. Pirandello's enthusiasm as he scans the horizon from west to east, taking in the Rocciavré Valley and its landmark talc mine, the Garida, then the Indritto Valley where the Sangonetto stream flows unbroken down to the small village of Giaveno through one of its many picturesque geological courses, is palpable—his sense of wonder, we might suppose, awakened by the stark contrast between this setting and his native Sicily, where African winds blow across subtropical, arid countryside.

But an even greater disparity for Pirandello was that between the city and country (or civilization and the wild). He was conscious of the city's encroachment on his beloved Alpine wilderness, registering his disdain for industrialization and its deleterious effect on the beauty of the landscape. In his fiction, Rome and his rustic birthplace of Agrigento are often represented as two halves of a conceptual dichotomy, where the latter is always threatened with moral contamination by the former. A common nineteenth-century trope, this rural/urban dyad is staged in Pirandello's stories against the backdrop of many unnamed landscapes where the conflict between innocence and corruption is played out. Thus, the *Coazze Notebook* imbues physical space with spiritual significance. Through it, Pirandello encounters his deepest feelings, and more importantly, cultivates a vision of nature as a silent observer and participant in human sorrows.

In his 1902 short story "Quando ero matto" ("When I Was Crazy"), written soon after the Coazze trip, Pirandello builds on the relationship between man and nature: its protagonist is literally unified with nature—his body has the shape of a tree, with branches for arms and underground rivers for his veins. Just as Pirandello had done in Coazze, the character adjusts his mood to the vicissitudes of nature: when, for instance, the wind tosses his leafy crown, his soul shudders. One can imagine Pirandello on his walks along the Alpine trails wrapped in blissful silence and brushed by the crisp air, attaining that level of harmony. Such moments are painstakingly recorded in his notebook.

The geography of a place, as Pirandello saw it, constitutes more than just its physical sphere. Man stays grounded by forging an emotional connection with the environment. Its profound influence can only be understood in terms of its grandeur and man's smallness. This idea had already been captured in Pirandello's 1894 short story "Rimedio: la geografia" ("Remedy: Geography"), whose protagonist imagines himself in a vastly different place on earth, learning to cure his malaise through imaginative identification. The aptly titled story conceives of man as powerless before the enormity of the cosmos. Human problems, in this view, are relatively trivial; they find their resolution in the universe's wisdom.

Pirandello's strolls in the Coazze woods no doubt stimulated these reflections. As his notes suggest, the natural world conveyed to him a form of visual and emotional knowledge tantamount to artistic inspiration. By losing himself in nature, he could access the fullness of his imagination—and, by extension, he could more fully understand the relationship between man and nature. Indeed, when Pirandello's characters find themselves in the natural world, and they attune themselves to it, its influence on them effects a self-transformation. On the other hand, characters caught in the clutches of time and history, as in Pirandello's 1913 novel *The Old and the Young*, find themselves perpetually disenchanted with life.

Pirandello's attachment to the Romantic idea of interconnection between nature and imagination is clearly evident in his notes, particularly when he describes his altered states of consciousness. He often seems to daydream as he stands on rock ledges, leaning on his walking stick and gazing at the horizon like a figure in a Caspar David Friedrich painting. These moments have a transcendent quality akin to those captured in Romantic poems about thundering waterfalls and mountain peaks. Like them, they are rooted in the senses. Pirandello acknowledges, for instance, the coldness of the stones he rests on. He sees a group of "stony" clouds lumbering off a mountain. Around him he hears a chorus of disparate sounds: bells announcing a Mass or the end of a workday; gusts of wind; trilling water; raindrops. Absorbing everything, he falls into ecstatic contemplation and lingers on the threshold of conscious awareness. Later, he will rhapsodize about this intense form of "solemnity," this harmonious connection with nature. That same feeling of "divine" unity will be invoked in his story, "When I Was Crazy," and then again in a theoretical context, in *On Humor* (1908), which elaborates on the "exceptional moment" in which man imaginatively engages with nature.

The influence that Coazze exerted on Pirandello's imagination is discernible throughout his work, and often explicitly in his poetry. His poem "Cargiore," published in 1903 in *La Riviera Ligure*, is a heartfelt ode to Coazze and the incomparable verdure and majestic silence of its Alpine valleys, interrupted only by the sound of streaming water and the change of seasons. For an artist who saw himself first as a poet, then as a writer of fiction, the opportunities for connecting so deeply with nature must have had enormous emotional significance. As the scattered verses in the *Notebook* show, feelings flowed out of Pirandello with Wordsworthian gusto.

THE COAZZE NOTEBOOK AS SOURCE TEXT

If the *Coazze Notebook* is, in part, a logbook for recording ecstatic experiences, it is also a sourcebook for Pirandello's fiction. Throughout, we find words, phrases, character sketches, and scenic descriptions that have their echo in later stories and plays. For example, a local resident named "Mr. Prever," who sometimes accompanied Pirandello on his hikes, appears as a character in Pirandello's 1902 short story, "Gioventù" ("Youth"), set in Coazze. That same Mr. Prever would come back in Pirandello's 1911 novel *Suo marito* (*Her Husband*), set partly in Coazze, though here renamed Cargiore. Chapters IV and VII, in particular, rely heavily on Pirandello's notes, as seen in the description of Silvia's living room and the Alpine refuge where she moves to cope with loss and to regain artistic inspiration. Cargiore is also the birthplace of Silvia's husband, her literary agent, and a major character in the narrative, who represents the tension between urban life (the locus of arid rhetoric) and the remote mountain hamlet which protects and fosters the artist's vision. Interestingly, Pirandello permitted only one edition of the novel in an effort to ward off accusations that he appropriated details from Grazia Deledda's marriage and professional life. In fact, he intended to rewrite the story from scratch, shifting the plot's focus to Silvia's husband and renaming the novel *Giustino Roncella nato Boggiòlo (Giustino Roncella Born Boggiòlo)*. However, Pirandello couldn't bring the rewritten plot to a conclusion. His son Stefano re-published the novel in 1941 with the partially altered chapters and the abridged title.

The influence of Coazze is felt not only in the symbolic patterning of the novel, but also in the characters' alienation. With her Sicilian roots and rejection of traditional standards, Silvia is Pirandello's alter ego; like him, she has the same "little demon" inside her pushing her towards a literary career, despite all odds. But Pirandello is also Giustino: deeply frustrated with his marriage and stifled by his wife. The complications of being an artist and being married are brought into greater relief by the novel's setting. Like Coazze, Cargiore is remote from urban society, forcing the characters to confront their problems. But that isolation and solitude are also vital for artistic and personal flourishing, as Pirandello himself recognizes in the *Coazze Notebook*. The need for separation from the practical matters of everyday life, Pirandello felt, was a precondition for his art. His ecstatic immersion in the natural world suggests the urgency of that need.

Previous editions of the *Coazze Notebook* hint at a possible connection between Pirandello's stay in the Alps and two short stories inspired by it, "Le medaglie" ("The Medals," 1904) and "Il sonno del vecchio" ("The Old Man's Slumber," 1906). Pirandello seems to have written them with specific people in mind, though no explicit references are made. Nonetheless, the stories clearly enact social dramas featuring characters and particular emotional responses that appear to be sourced from real life. Pirandello would surely have witnessed local community gatherings and taken note of their social dynamics, seeing how the narrow-mindedness of its members paralleled the town's social constraints and lack of intellectual exchange.

In the 1907 "Dal naso al cielo" ("From Nose to Sky"), the material world is implicated in the conflict between imagination and scientific knowledge. Highly visual in its narrative structure, the tale draws on macabre imagery to illustrate the quest for free thinking, particularly against the disdainful scientist, Romualdo Reda, who repudiates imagination. When Reda dies beneath a chestnut tree, a spider spins a web between the tree's branches and the scientist's large nose, here symbolizing the limited scope of academic knowledge. The spider is resolved to leave and find more open space, a gothic metaphor for the trajectory of the imagination, or the emancipation of art.

The *Notebook* is remarkable for its one-to-one correspondence between real life and fiction. It is impossible to overlook how closely Pirandello's experiences and feelings parallel his creative thinking. The sharpness of his details—about individual lives, habits, appearances, behaviors, and modes of self-expression—betrays the keenness of his observation and his insistence on crafting realistic plots and creating believable characters. In fact, Coazze's residents became the models for Pirandello's art, and he would transcribe them into his fiction in all their complexity and peculiarity. For instance, we find the *Generalessa*, whose body shape and temperament would serve as a model for a female character in the 1905 short story "Di guardia" ("Watch and Ward"). In the 1902 short story "Gioventù" ("Youth"), Mr. Grattarola, the owner of Coazze's drugstore, has been turned into Monsù Grattarola, the owner of a pharmacy-post office, exactly as Pirandello had plotted it in his notes. Similarly, in the 1905 short story "La messa di quest'anno" ("This Year's Mass")—a kind of elegy for the forgotten spirit of Christmas and its roots in love and charity—the protagonist arrives in Cargiore from Rome to visit his Aunt Velia, a character modeled on one of Pirandello's real acquaintances in Coazze. The train ride itself parallels the playwright's own journey from Rome to the hamlet. Upon his arrival, the man will find the Alpine community thrown into disarray by the local priest's overly "logical" interpretation of the Christmas spirit. By taking the idea of renunciation too literally, the priest turns Christmas into a somber, frustrating, and austere holiday. Pirandello himself despised this form of Christian zeal and rationalism. The story was included in the collection *Beffe della morte e della vita* (*Jests of Life and Death*), which Pirandello gave his sister as a Christmas present upon returning from Coazze. The dedication read: "To Lina and Calogero in memory of a month of blissful peace."[5]

VISUAL ART IN THE *COAZZE NOTEBOOK*

For Pirandello, real-life situations and places, real people, their speech habits, and their behaviors constituted a virtual laboratory from which he could draw inspiration and test ideas – the Pirandellian *modus operandi* critics are so fond of pointing out. By the same token, the drawings contained in the text serve an equally important function in Pirandello's art, rendering ideas for stories in visual form. Most conspicuous is the illustration of the main church in Coazze with its bell tower and inscription, "Each in His Own Way."[6] A gesture of religious tolerance at a time

---

[5] Dated December 22, 1901, the handwritten dedication is featured in the original volume of collected short stories preserved in Pirandello's personal library in his studio in Rome.

[6] Upon entering Coazze, one sees the church of Santa Maria del Pino, with its bell tower and iconic inscription "Ognuno a Suo Modo" ("Each in his own way"), overlooking the town square. The inscription not only suggests the hamlet's liberality but also distinguishes the church from another nearby, the Chapel of the Confraternity (perhaps the parish

when Coazze had a sizable community of Waldensians, the sign became the title for Pirandello's play which premiered in Milan at the *Teatro dei Filodrammatici* in May 1924.

Each in His Own Way underscores the arbitrary nature of truth and the ambiguity of interpretation and opinion. Like the maxim on the Coazze bell tower, the play celebrates individual freedom and autonomy, even to the point of inviting the audience to join in the performance (if spectators "chose" to). The play's "choral interludes," as Pirandello referred to them, blurred the boundary between truth and fiction, mixing up characters on the stage with "real" people in the lobby. This unraveling of the layered interplay of art and reality obliquely parallels the cognitive dissonance inherent in the bell tower's inscription. Moreover, it dramatizes the reciprocity of mimesis: art mirroring life, and life mirroring art. By collapsing the fourth wall, Pirandello was able to challenge accepted notions of truth, revealing the ways in which it is constructed in the nuanced interplay of art and reality, fact and interpretation. The origins of these reflections are to be found, of course, in the *Coazze Notebook*, where they were allowed to mature over two decades.

Pirandello's illustrations reflect on the one hand, his Romantic faith in art as a medium of the imagination, and on the other, his neoclassical insistence on imitating nature: the visionary intertwined with the representational. His drawing of the bell tower, for one, is striking in its verisimilitude, especially in the way the belfry peeks out from the residential

---

church at one time), which did not seem to be as tolerant of the Waldesians.

area and is overshadowed by the mountains. It has the exactness of a snapshot. Landscapes and architectural sketches recur most frequently, not just in the *Coazze Notebook*, but in all of his visual artwork. When he painted (usually *en plein air*), his favorite subject was the landscape. Produced with thick, rapid brushstrokes, his landscape paintings gave form to places that were close to his heart and which he wanted to fix in his memory.

The intermixing of imagination and representation can also be seen in Pirandello's sketch of a medieval building, isolated in the middle of a page towards the end of the *Notebook*. Unlike the bell tower, it cannot be traced to a recognizable source. It seems, rather, like an exercise in style or simply the product of the artist's wandering mind, predisposed to seeing stories in objects rather than in incidents. Whether this drawing can be linked to any of Pirandello's tales is debatable since no date or specific detail is given. Its significance, however, lies outside the scope of mere visual representation; it is an attempt to endow the sketch with literary value. Indeed, the drawings in the *Notebooks* show Pirandello grappling with his own distress and looking for ways to make sense of life through his art, as well as to fill in the gaps between reality and imagination— a struggle for equanimity and meaning that preoccupied him throughout his career.

This latter point is significant in understanding Pirandello's penchant for visualizing his thoughts and transforming them into narrative patterns. Doodling in the margins or sketching out pictures helped him think, allowing him to liberate his creative impulses and plumb the depths of his unconscious. A devoted painter all his life, he regarded visual art as a powerful means of emotional expression. Scholars have even found a correlation between his canvases and his literary work, both of which reflect a significant degree of self-examination. The drawings in the *Coazze Notebook* should therefore not be underestimated. On the contrary, they are deeply introspective exercises, as well as attempts to transfigure places or moments that left a deep impression on him.

Pirandello's sketches serve one other under-recognized function: they foreshadow his conceptualization of comedy, as articulated in his seminal essay "On Humor" (1908). In the same vein, they were a coping mechanism that helped him make sense of life. The drawing of a clown in the *Notebook's* final pages is a good example. Next to the clown is the figure of a man, his head tilted pensively, and his eyes and facial expression heavily shaded over in pencil. This juxtaposition of the comical and melancholic illustrates not just Pirandello's own divided state, but what he saw as the human condition, which he described as "humoristic." The humor lies in man's desperate but sympathetic state. When he describes "the feeling of the opposite" produced through the activity of reflection, he is referring to an irreconcilable condition that man must come to terms with. But instead of explaining that condition discursively, he visualizes it as the paradoxical combination of "both a violin and a double bass."

LANGUAGE IN THE *COAZZE NOTEBOOK*

If landscapes dominate the *Notebook*'s first part, the second is preoccupied with language and its generative power. The Tuscan dialect, so fascinating to Pirandello, lavishes his text with a rich visualism, a charming interplay of image and metaphor. We can see, moreover, how Pirandello used Tuscan expressions in his fiction, weaving them into such short stories as "Il vitalizio" ("The Annuity"), "Il fumo" ("The Fumes"), "Acqua Amara" ("Bitter Waters"), "Pallino e Mimì" ("Pallino and Mimì"), "La balia" ("The Wet Nurse"), and "Spunta un giorno" ("A Day Dawns"). Written between 1903 and the 1930s, these stories also show how indelible the melodic regionalisms of Montepulciano were in Pirandello's memory.

Since as early as the 1890s, when he was writing his doctoral thesis on Agrigentino, Pirandello was preoccupied with language. His main concern throughout his artistic career was to escape the clutches of rhetoric and mannerism, which he felt precluded vivid and authentic characterization. Manzoni's novels showed him a new way forward; in them he saw the origin of a common language that could live, breathe, and speak in different registers. By mixing the standard language with the verve of local dialects, an author could add dimension to characters and define unique points of view. Nuances in language, as Pirandello saw it, produced nuances in culture.

Thus, it isn't surprising that he turned so faithfully to the notes he took in Coazze and Montepulciano to help shape his characters and their dialogue. Pirandello's characters move and speak as if they were carved out of aphorisms and popular legends, their personalities drawn from the eccentric figures Pirandello had met. His notes offer not only the opportunity to understand how he worked but also evidence that his characters had real-life counterparts. Although the Montepulciano notes are narrow in scope, their significance in Pirandello's fiction is abundantly clear. They show us that what might be mistaken for pure invention was in fact an imaginary reworking of direct experience.

The significance of regional dialects in Pirandello's art cannot be overstated, especially in terms of the playwright's commitment to realism. If art and life were for him interchangeable, then his use of language had the spontaneity of actual speech. This was one principle that he adhered to throughout his career, rejecting the rhetorical bravura of D'Annunzio in favor of a more colloquial style reminiscent of Giovanni Verga's *verismo*. Even during the surreal period of his final years, when naturalism yielded to irony and pessimism, his narrative technique never departed from the needs of realistic characterization.

Pirandello's attention to linguistic detail was almost fanatical. For example, when his fiction ventures into cinematography (still a burgeoning field at the time), he employs a highly specialized idiom which he picked up by carefully observing the interaction of actors and director in film studios. Despite his Sicilian roots and lack of familiarity with the Tuscan dialect, he reworked the expressions he heard with impressive competence, especially as seen in the stories written after Montepulciano. In some of them, for instance, Pirandello displays a stunning command of very specific vernacular words, such as *bertuccia* and *sbertucciare*, which he converts from their derogatory connotation of "monkey" – a reference to a bland, ugly woman (cf. "Donna Mimma," "Guardando una stampa" ["Looking at a Print"], "Il dovere del medico" ["The Doctor's Duty"]) – to something like "ragged" and "worn out," as seen in the novel *The Old and the Young* and the comedy *Man, Beast, and Virtue*.

No less remarkable was Pirandello's ability to invoke his native Sicily while, at the same time, deploying Florentine expressions, as we see in the 1904 short story "Il fumo" ("The Fumes"). Building on the concept of "taking possession" (from the Tuscan phrase which he heard in Montepulciano), the tale focuses on the harsh life of miners in Sicily's sulfur mines—a life Pirandello knew well from working in his father's mine as a young man. Tuscan expressions abound in the story, reinforcing the contrast between the authenticity of the country with the inhumanity of industry.

For Pirandello, realism transcended faithful descriptions of characters and settings. A realistic representation had to evoke a living language, one used by real people in real-life situations. As Antonio Gramsci pointed out in reviews of Pirandello's plays, the spoken language and its vernacular expressions, as the playwright used them, enabled audiences to identify with the characters. He added that Pirandello's art cannot be fully comprehended if we overlook those "rustic" nuances.

This emphasis on spoken language became a hallmark of Pirandello's art, especially in his novellas. Indeed, his tales abound in the vernacular, cropping up in interior monologues, rhetorical questions, exclamations and interjections, repetition, and hesitations. Dialogue, in particular, is a critical aspect of Pirandello's fiction. Both highly evocative and colloquial, it reflects his insistence on verisimilitude. While he was often criticized for being too cerebral, a charge that weighed heavily on him, Pirandello was adamant about his true-to-life style, which he honed by exploring questions of identity and truth, as well as the contours of human consciousness. And it was apparent as early as 1901 when he was writing his Coazze notes.

Through Pirandello's habit of dramatizing his own experiences, we can see how he transformed the facts of everyday life and the peculiarities of ordinary people into the substance of his work. At the same time, the *Coazze Notebook* shows us Pirandello, in the earliest stage of his career, methodically and persistently searching for a mode of stylistic and linguistic expression all his own.

INTRODUCING THE *COAZZE NOTEBOOK* TO ANGLOPHONE READERS

This translation of the *Coazze Notebook* is the first attempt to introduce Pirandello's notebooks to an anglophone readership. Together with *Taccuino di Bonn*, *Taccuino segreto*, and *Taccuino di Harvard* (all published only in Italian), the *Coazze Notebook* testifies to Pirandello's keen observations of the world around him, while also showing how his art was nourished by his copious notes and reflections on daily life.[7] The *Coazze Notebook* thus situates itself in a wider corpus of notes which remains largely unavailable to English-language readers.

The playwright's vacations in the Alps and the Tuscan countryside anticipate other retreats in the years to come, such as those in Soriano del Cimino, Anticoli Corrado, and Alatri, whose ambience and rustic charm proved fruitful for creative work. The notebooks Pirandello kept during these trips all bear witness to the inspiring influence of these locales.

---

[7] Parts of the *Taccuino di Bonn* were published by Corrado Alvaro in "Nuova Antologia" on January 1, 1934; *Taccuino segreto*, edited by Annamaria Andreoli (Milan: Mondadori, 1997); *Taccuino di Harvard*, edited by Ombretta Frau and Cristina Gragnani (Milan: Mondadori, 2002).

Moreover, all are similar in content and style—personal reflections and moody sentiments intermingling with drafts of literary criticism, poems, and sketches—though the *Coazze Notebook* is, in graphical terms, one of the richest among them. The similarities between the notebooks suggests that Pirandello's summer retreats engendered a particular kind of thought pattern.

In addition to making the notes accessible to a broader audience, this translation also sheds light on Pirandello's writing life. It shows how the playwright processed his emotions and impressions, and how he developed his unique narrative style. We can see how he fleshed out his ideas in fictional plotlines, laying the groundwork for his plays. Despite the challenges of rendering regional dialect and vernacular into English, this translation faithfully transcribes Pirandello's feelings and literary ambition from as early as 1901, when his reputation as a major Italian modernist was not yet established.

Central to the *Coazze Notebook* is the relationship between language and translation. As an awed beholder of Alpine scenery, Pirandello uses poetic diction to articulate his childlike wonder; as a curious observer of Coazze society and its regionalisms, he endeavors to faithfully reproduce what he sees and hears, much like an anthropologist. This translation strives to preserve Pirandello's own *translations,* of his experience of the natural world and of local culture. At the same time, it recognizes the fraught nature of translation, just as Pirandello had. While it may serve as a bridge between languages, cultures, or experiences, translation is also, inevitably, a process of alteration. Pirandello reflected extensively on this fact, perhaps most explicitly in his 1908 essay

"Illustrators, Actors, and Translators." As he saw it, the author's original "creation" (and his intention, we might add) is "betrayed" when a work is translated—an artist's defense of the purity and uniqueness of the creative act.

At the risk of "betraying" Pirandello's work, the notes had to undergo partial adjustments, especially wherever a literal translation would have been less comprehensible to an English-language reader. This is most evident in the notes Pirandello took in Montepulciano: basically, a list of dialectal expressions somewhat detached from a specific narrative context. Some of the proverbs and colorful sayings that he found so captivating had to be adapted; otherwise, one gets a mashup of words that may sound correct in isolation but are meaningless when brought together in English. Only in a few instances did the Montepulciano dialect prove untranslatable. Such was the case with words like *roccia* (Tuscan for *dirt,* in contrast to its standard Italian equivalent, *rock*), which were left in their original form. No alternative expression in English would have conveyed these words' resonance. The footnotes serve to fill in the gaps and to show how regional diversity is refracted in language.

The process of translation was often twofold, with significant attention paid to cultural context: one translation rendered the Tuscan into standard Italian, and another turned the standard Italian into English. We can imagine Pirandello himself performing this linguistic trans-codification, as some of the expressions he encountered in Montepulciano would indeed have been incomprehensible even to a native Italian speaker. (It is worth bearing in mind that Italian dialects differ so markedly from each other that a speaker of one will often sound unintelligible to that of another.) To preserve this sense of foreignness, which Pirandello very likely experienced, some words have been left in the original Tuscan, accompanied by detailed footnotes explaining the sociocultural differences in etymology. In addition to providing the reader with context for the notes, this approach aims to show the ways in which Pirandello skillfully negotiated those differences and even adopted certain expressions that recur in his work.

By its nature, translation modifies its source, but it also allows the dissemination of cultural knowledge of the text by adapting it to the tastes of the target culture. To those who believe that translation permits literature to travel across historical, linguistic, and cultural chasms, Pirandello will come to life. And to those who don't, the image of the future Nobel laureate bent over his notebook in the Alps, trying to distill from his scattered notes and reflections a coherent narrative, will nevertheless reveal itself in all its charm.

If nothing else, the *Coazze Notebook* is a picture of Pirandello at the outset of his literary career, moved to keen observation and reflection by the surrounding world. In quiet contemplation, he turned to his notebook to record daily experiences, to explore ideas and develop plots, to draw, and even to write poetry—and in doing so, to grapple with the tensions of real life. For all its eccentricities, the notebook documents the formation of an artist.

The Coazze Notebook

Coazze in Valsusa. Surrounded by mountains. End of August, it's green everywhere, just as in May. Meadows are watered. Ready for a second round of mowing. The grass grows back after just two days. The village is teeming with people and the sound of water running through the *zane*.[1] On the other side is the old cathedral. The Sangone Valley.[2] Chestnut woods.

Coazze Bell Tower

[1] In its regional nuances, the word *zana* (Pirandello is here using the noun in the plural) has come to mean both a shallow oval-shaped woven basket and a depression in the ground where water can easily stagnate. In the mountains, however, a *zana* is a fissure within rocks through which water flows. The term was originally introduced by the Lombards (who called it *zain(j)ā*), after they invaded Italy from modern western Hungary and ruled the peninsula for almost two centuries (from 568 to 774 AD). They also used the term to refer to a basket for carrying goods, like our modern backpack, or *zaino* in Italian, which clearly resembles the Lombard word. Pirandello incorporated the *zana* in his fiction, most notably in tales such as "Gioventù" ("Youth," 1902) and "Di guardia" ("Watch and Ward," 1905), both set in mountain villages analogous to Coazze: Cargiore and Gore, respectively. Cargiore and Gore are fictional names for Coazze.

[2] The Sangone Valley is named after the Sangone River; it starts in the Cottian Alps and runs through the lands between the Val di Susa (north) and the Val Chisone (south). The river then flows through the villages of Coazze and Giaveno, as Pirandello noted, before entering the plain of Turin and finally merging into the Po River, the longest river in Italy. Pirandello's description is from the perspective of Coazze. The Sangone Valley is mentioned in "Marsina stretta" ("The Tight Frock Coat"), a short story Pirandello composed during his stay in Coazze. In fact, the story was published in *Il Marzocco* on December 1, 1901.

The Cathedral bell. The octagonal spire. One double-lancet window. Clock - "Each in His Own Way"[3] - D.O.M. ET B.M.V. SIDERA SCANDENTI.[4]

- Prever - Martino Prever.[5]

p. 1238

- The clouds and the mountains - Big clouds turned to stone - Mountains of air - (black mountains of air - stifling - gloomy.) -

Other mountains, their sides engulfed in fog - or in a vaporous purple shade.

- A quiver in the silence - chirping crickets[6] - laughing streams -

- The solemnity of shadow-wrapped mountains - A swarm of swallows almost hugging the meadows.

- Steep and gloomy gorges shaded by dwarf alder trees.

- Chestnut coppice and alder trees.

---

[3] The origins of the inscription are unknown, though it might have been added when the bell tower was constructed in 1575. Over time, it descended to the ground as the tower's foundation settled, reinforcing the contrast with the adjoining cathedral. According to legend, the local Waldensians made the inscription as a statement of religious tolerance. Oddly, no such message appears on the façade of the nearby Waldensian church. Pirandello's 1924 play, *Each in His Own Way*, is part of the "theatre in the theatre" trilogy, alongside *Six Characters in Search of an Author* and *Tonight We Improvise*. The play concerns the arbitrariness of appearance.

[4] Deo Optimo Maximo et Beata Maria Vergine Sidera Scandenti ("To God, the best and greatest and the blessed Virgin Mary, who ascends to the stars). The same image of the Virgin Mary is portrayed in the fourth chapter of Pirandello's novel *Her Husband* (*Suo marito*), which features a local church with an "octagonal spire" and "double-lancet windows."

[5] The name of a character in the 1902 short story "Gioventù" ("Youth"). In it, Martino Prever commits suicide out of despair of ever being with his beloved Velia and is buried in the local cemetery.

[6] Pirandello uses the word *zighi* to refer to chirping. The term comes from the onomatopoeic verb *zigare* which phonetically reproduces the short, high-pitched sound made by some animals. Pirandello might have heard the word during his sojourn in Piedmont, where it appears in the local dialects. However, *zigare* is also a poetic verb. The poet Giosuè Carducci, whom Pirandello admired, described the sound a rabbit makes as *zighi*.

Little foaming waterfalls - The water runs through the gorges; has already irrigated a meadow - runs blessedly to do good elsewhere.

Sunday, August 25th

A humid, ash-grey veiled sky - The closest woods appear gloomy; the farthest ones fade away in the fog, annoyed - Villagers leave the cathedral herd-like after Mass; first the men, then the women. They have pondered the state of their souls and perhaps their mortality; now life reclaims them: they begin chatting, happy to hear their voices in the fresh morning air after the solemnity of worship.

- Alpine morning - Up in the mountains - The festiveness of the valley.

- A shepherd's cottage

Types. General C. - A retired general - 68-years-old. Long goatee and thick, grey moustache. Bold, robust, thin legs; stands with a cane. Beautiful dark eyes, a nice nose: Jewish. Energetic and candid: he tells you to your face what he has to say - unceremoniously; but he is polite. You can see him sitting pensively in front of his modest cottage, wearing a white canvas cap with a leather visor, his cane between his legs; the garden walls are topped by an iron fence. A few wild flowerbeds; a few messy plants. He has a son, Poldo, a good-looking, ten-year-old boy who, the General thinks, should be raised like a military cadet; but he is spoiled: an only child.

The *Generalessa* has something about her.[7] A beautiful woman, in her fifties; a bit plump.[8] She claims to have a heart condition, but you couldn't tell. Maybe she hides it

---

[7] A *generalessa* is the mother general of a convent. Here, the name refers to the General's wife.

[8] The Generalessa is described similarly in the short story "Di guardia" ("Watch and Ward"), written in 1905 shortly after Pirandello's stay in Coazze.

well with makeup: she uses mascara, and you can tell. According to the town gossips, she started out as the General's maid. But she talks about her father who had a good position and salary. Her brother is the director of a bus company in Florence. Her father gave her away to a count when she was eighteen. She was up to all sorts of things. She had to serve the count for eight years. "The count and his disease of the spinal cord! But he was a count ... As a widow, still beautiful (I don't say this in vain), I met the General; the suitors were visiting; he was a handsome soldier and we fell in love; it ended how it was supposed to." Poldino was born; she knew how to do things properly: a wet nurse suckled the baby; they got married.

She cooks for the General. She is from Naples but speaks Piedmontese fluently. When speaking Italian, she likes to sprinkle her speech with regional expressions; to be more effective, she uses Piedmontese. Her gestures are feeble, as if her hands were frail. There, there, if she really was a countess, she is too proud now to be the General's lady. And this makes you think that she really was a maid. After all, she is very courteous.

September 4th

It's a gloomy, foggy, rainy morning. Raindrops fall from the iron railing. Veils of fog scattered along the mountainside. A cloudy, heavy sky.[9] Among the acacia and chestnut trees, a few birds seem to call for help.

Types – L. Prever: old, tall, good-looking; long gray beard, almost white; he wears a canvas cap.[10] He's a billionaire but enjoys the company of poor people. A philanthro-

[9] Compare this with the description of the weather in "Gioventù" ("Youth"),which mirrors the emotional atmosphere of the scene when Velia's family gathers around her deathbed.

[10] The exact same description will be used in the novel *Her Husband* for the characterization of Monsù Prever, the old, rich man secretly in love with Madame Velia Boggiolo, the protagonist's mother.

pist – he built and furnished a kindergarten. Owns a cottage in Coazze and a detached villa on the top of Colle di Braida, in the Valgioje valley, from which you can glimpse the magnificent Valsusa. Despite his philanthropy, Coazze didn't re-elect him mayor. Maybe that's why he steers clear of the "good people." At any rate, he never leaves the village, not even in the winter.

Dr. Frangoro: tall, thin, with blonde whiskers and white hair; cold, silent, put together. He also owns a gray cottage, with a large backyard. Has a nice wife and three or four children. Lives up here in the winter. I can only imagine what the winter must be like in these foggy mountains, with these meadows that are now so green but soon to be covered with snow; the skeleton trees... What will the doctor be doing in January? The pharmacist is his enemy. He has something about him, this Mr. Grattarola. He's got a stiff leg and limps. Short, yellow-skinned; white eyes and Chinese-style whiskers; quiet, annoyed, unpleasant. He's the local shopkeeper and the post office is also in his pharmacy.[11] Only during fixed hours of operation can you ask him for a letter. He won't do anyone any favors. Sometimes, he doesn't even take care of the doctor's preparations, forcing the doctor to send them to Giaveno. Each one calls the other a *chiel* (*donkey* in Piedmontese).[12]

Mrs. Spingardi: The Colonel's wife. Her husband is always missing; must have married her for her fortune. She's 13 or 15 years older, and a widow with two old daughters from a previous marriage; one of them is even married.

September 5th – Sun, will you triumph over this smoky, oppressive night? Drive it away to those foggy mountains. But the night is too dense and heavy, and your light shines

[11] In "Gioventù," the character Monsù Grattarola owns a shop that doubles as a pharmacy and post office. *Monsù* means *mister* in the Coazze dialect.

[12] In "Gioventù," Madame Velia uses the word *chiel* when she shouts at her son: "Ch' a vada via chiel!" ("Go away, donkey!").

too faintly over there. The poplars and acacias seem to be straightening up from the dewy meadows as though to witness the battle. They would be happy if one of your rays, like a long sword, ploughed through the hostile vapor; but alas, it all seems as black as night.

- The tall lady – dark – skinny – always by her husband's side.

- In September, daisies blanket the meadows. It looks like snow.

- The Braida hill.[13] Cherry trees. Beech trees, chestnut trees, alder trees, birch trees.

- Along the Giaveno Boulevard: chestnut trees and turkey oaks. On Buffa Street, the loud running water.

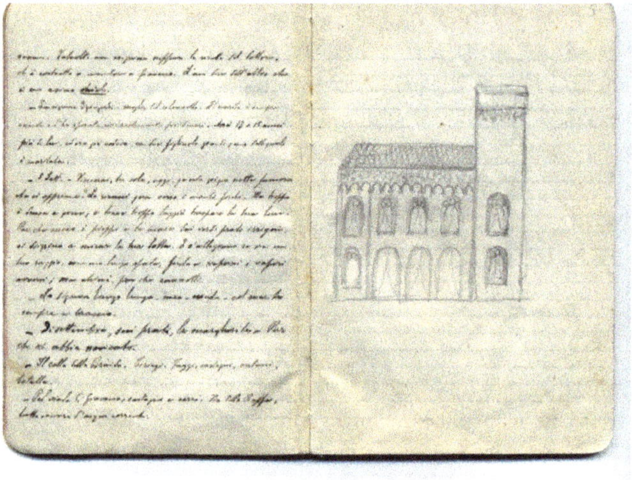

Pencil drawing of a medieval building

[13] Colle Braida, as it is called in Italian, is a mountain crossing in the Alps, between Val di Susa and Val Sangone. Braida Hill can be reached from both Avigliana (in Val di Susa) and Giaveno (in Val Sangone). The latter route leads to the small village of Valgioie, which Pirandello mentions in his notes, indicating what path he took. The area's dense beechwood forest is still a popular destination for hiking. It is also renowned for its large mushroom patch. In fact, one of the main branches of the local mycology school is located here.

- Like the three Parcae, three old ladies sit under a chestnut tree, spinning wool and watching cows.
- Between the rocks in the river.

September 14th
- The Sangonetto Torrent, in the Indritto Valley, flows into the Sangone which runs down the Forno Valley. The largest part runs through the channel - There, the water gushes noisily, swirls, foams between the rocks; here, it is placid, running through the duct before being pressed into industry.[14]
- Up to a height of 3,280 ft, the area is covered with chestnut trees - Between 3,280 ft and 6,560 ft, there are birch trees, beech trees, fir trees, Scots pine trees, and larch trees. Between 6,560 ft and 8,202 ft, only mountain meadow. Beyond 6,560 ft, there is no vegetation.
- A velvety hedge of chestnut trees, between the Sangone on one side and Rio Fronteglio on the other. Casale Inverso.[15]
- Frainet[16] - (Hamlets: Villareto, Galleana, Fornello, Selvaggio, Ruadamonte, Rufinera, Mattonera, Pian del Viermo,

---

[14] The Sangonetto Torrent is one of the major tributaries of the River Sangone. It flows from the montane region of Coazze and merges into the Sangone River in the vicinity of Borgata Sangonetto, the tiny hamlet near Coazze named after the Sangonetto. Pirandello is here describing the picturesque region bordering the Indritto and the Forno Valleys, a mining area at the time. In the late nineteenth century, companies received permits to survey the areas around Forno and Indritto, as well as the water basin around the Sangonetto. Excavations occurred over several decades and led to the construction of the first mine gallery (the "Vecchia Garida"), followed by a second in 1925 (the "Nuova Garida"). Talc mining soon became a major industry in the area. One of the oldest mines in the Alps, the Garida, is now open to the public and offers a glimpse into mining life in the beginning of the twentieth century. Pirandello was deeply conscious of the encroachment of industry upon the area's natural beauty.
[15] A description of the Sangone Valley. Bordered by the Sangone River and stretching out approximately fifteen miles along the western side of Piedmont, the Sangone Valley descends into the slopes of the Cottian Alps, which divide France and Italy. It's no surprise that Pirandello's attention was captured by the leafy and verdant paths that separate the Sangone from the Fronteglio, a woodland full of chestnut trees and shady walking trails.
[16] The name of one of Coazze's neighboring hamlets.

Brando, Savoja, Viretta, Balangero, Cargiore, Rolando, etc.).[17]

- Mountains: Roccia Corba, Monte Luzera, Costa del Pagliaio, Uja, Cugno dell'Alpet, Brunello, Roccia Vrè, Rubinett.

Cargiore - not Frainet.

Oh, mystery of the gloomy gorges / under the thick, glaucous alders.

Opposite, looking south, is Mount Bocciarda.

At 6:00 am, the bell summons the parishioners. Down in the valley, a long, plaintive whistle calls the workers to the factories - At dawn, the western mountains are covered with snow - To the east, high on the hill, the sacred Superga.[18]

1902

January *Riviera Ligure*[19]	Liras	25.00
"*Nuova Antologia*: "Lontano" ("Far Away")[20]	Liras	180.00

[17] Most of these hamlets appear in chapter 4 of Pirandello's novel *Her Husband*. The protagonist's familiarity with the region is contrasted with her emotional distance from it. Pirandello uses the desolate setting as a backdrop against which to stage Silvia's search for an authentic life and her struggles to reconcile her emotions.

[18] Pirandello's enthusiasm about the Sangone Valley is heightened by the views it affords, including that of the neoclassical Basilica of Superga in the Province of Turin (now the Metropolitan City of Turin).

[19] Letters between Pirandello and Mario Novaro, the director of *La Riviera Ligure*, indicate Pirandello's assiduous collaboration with the Ligurian literary journal. Between 1900 and 1905, Pirandello submitted at least two works of either poetry or short fiction per year, hence the recurring payment of 25 liras in the list. To read the letters, see Luigi Pirandello, *Carteggi inediti*, edited by Sarah Zappulla Muscarà, Quaderni dell'Istituto di Studi Pirandelliani, n. 2, Roma: Bulzoni, 1980.

[20] The publication of this story in *Nuova Antologia* marks the beginning of Pirandello's long-lasting and fruitful collaboration with the prestigious Florentine literary journal. Practically a novella (it is divided into eleven chapters), "Lontano" ("Far Away") focuses on the conflict between a humble Sicilian girl and a Norwegian sailor, while offering a glimpse of Pirandello's native Sicily and life in the local *solfare* (sulfur mines). According to his calculations, the story yielded a considerable return, over six times more than Pirandello would receive for a single piece. In the same year, he published his second novel *Il turno* (*The Turn*),

February	*Riviera Ligure*	Liras	25.00
March	*Riviera Ligure*	Liras	25.00
April	*Zampogna* (*Bagpipes*)[21]	Liras	16.50
May	*Riviera Ligure*	Liras	25.00
June	Honorarium	Liras	197.00
July	Macerata[22]	Liras	132.00
			625.50

But harsher is the winter,
Heavy with dense fog and perennial snow.[23]

---

which he'd written in 1895, a second collection of short stories, titled *Beffe della morte e della vita* (*Jests of Life and Death*), and an anthology of fourteen tales, "Quando ero matto" ("When I Was Mad"). Despite these successes, Pirandello's income still depended heavily on the money he and his wife had invested in the family sulfur mine. When it was flooded the following year, the Pirandellos faced financial ruin and the loss of their patrimony.

[21] The collection of lyrical poems *Zampogna* (*Bagpipes*) was published in Rome in 1901 by the Società Editrice Dante Alighieri. Written between 1892 and 1899, the poems were inspired by Giovanni Pascoli's symbolist style. It is unclear why Pirandello reported his earnings from this work here. The sum may refer to his royalties.

[22] A quiet hill town in the Marche region where Pirandello often stayed. Macerata exerted a considerable influence on the author. In 1915, at a train station in Macerata, he parted with his son Stefano, who boarded a train for the Western Front. In 1917, also in Macerata, Pirandello wrote his comedy *Il piacere dell'onestà* (*The Pleasure of Honesty*). The town reappears in stories inspired by the atrocities of World War I, such as "Quando si comprende" ("War," 1918) and "Jeri e oggi" ("Yesterday and Today," 1919). In both stories, Macerata is where soldiers are stationed, and military convoys gather. However, it is unclear why Pirandello cites the town in his financial records. The adjacent sum could refer to his work as a college exam commissioner, a job he often took in the summer. It could also reflect his earnings from his submissions to literary journals.

[23] In the original manuscript, this verse is written in pencil on the very last page, detached from the rest of the notes. It was moved to the front of the text in the 1960 Mondadori edition (and consequently in this translation), presumably because of its association with Coazze. Elements of the verse reappear in the poem "Cargiore" (1903), which Pirandello published in the progressive literary journal, *La Riviera Ligure*. Divided into three parts, the poem celebrates the calming effect of the moon-lit landscape and the change of seasons on the speaker. Interestingly, the poem's second part (which incorporates this verse line) is featured in Pirandello's novel *Her Husband* as a lyric poem written by the protagonist, Silvia Roncella. In the novel, the landscape is a source of catharsis and creative inspiration; it assuages Silvia's grief over her child's death as it absorbs her in its grandeur. The poem is now part of *Poesie varie*, in *Saggi, Poesie e Scritti Varii*, edited by Manlio Lo Vecchio-Musti, Milan: Mondadori, 1965, pp. 825-7.

ꟸ[24]

A broad, serene view of cultivated lands: – Mount Amiata - Three lakes: two of them small (Montepulciano and Chiusi) - Trasimeno –

- A village buffeted by the winds (about 1,968 ft above sea level) - Father Innocenzo, a priest in the Collegiata, celebrates Mass in another parish, over at the Church of Our Lady of the Roses. Gives Latin lessons to high schoolers.

- Mount Amiata.

- Mrs. Naccheri, a widow, runs a boarding house. Tuscan hospitality - She has a daughter - abandoned by her husband - Father Innocenzo is this lady's cousin.

- A shortage of doctors in the winter

- Scorching hot today.[25] All the windows are shut

- Oh, girl, what do you think? They heard the bell and didn't come?

- Mount Cetuna[26] - The tower of the Sarteano Castle

- The Chiana Valley[27]

---

[24] The following notes, which appear directly after the Coazze notes, were likely written during Pirandello's 1903 stay in Montepulciano, a medieval hill town in southern Italy, situated between Florence and Siena. Carrying out his summer appointment as a college examiner, Pirandello delighted in the musicality of the Tuscan dialect. The *Montepulciano Notes*, as Pirandello scholars have dubbed them, are a long list of Tuscan expressions the playwright wrote down as he heard them used by the locals. These notes reflect not only Pirandello's interest in different dialects but also his keenness to have his characters speak in as natural and spontaneous a way as possible. The same Tuscan vernacular recurs in short stories like "Il vitalizio" ("The Annuity") and "Il Fumo" ("The Fumes").

[25] The vernacular expression "affogare dal caldo" literally means "the heat's drowning us." Pirandello was fascinated by such Tuscan idioms, which are often unintelligible to Italian speakers from other regions.

[26] Misspelling of Mount Cetona, located in southern Tuscany. Mount Cetona is a well-known starting point in many itineraries, easily accessed from the small villages of Cetona and Sarteano, which were popular attractions among the literati of the time like Pirandello, Carducci and Prezzolini.

[27] The Chiana Valley, situated between the provinces of Arezzo and Siena in Tuscany and the provinces of Perugia and Terni in Umbria, is the largest valley in the Apennine Mountains. Settled by the Etruscans and the Romans in the early third century BC, the Chiana Valley was considered the granary of Italy. When Hannibal raided the area in 217 BC, he was able to stock his entire army before his legendary crossing of the Alps and his victory in the Battle of Lake Trasimeno. Today, the

- *It don't bother us*[28] telling him, "You have to study, Ubaldino!"
- He writes "trito trito" in "crushed" letters (meaning, miniscule)
- The mother is pickier than the rest with her kids

The Marquise - a seamstress in her youth; the lover of Marquis D.G. (who was married). The poor Marquis has two daughters - one with his wife and one with his mistress. The wife dies and the Marquis marries the mistress - his daughter dies, and he inherits her mother's fortune. The Marquis dies and the Marquise inherits both his fortune and his dead wife's. A big, beautiful woman, mannish in demeanor and voice - big nose, olive-skinned - wears wire-rimmed glasses. She lives in the country and takes care of everything by herself.

- Oleographs paid for *a bit a month* in Magdalen Square
- He stuck the note in *the shutter*
- A girl *gone bad*: stuff for the war, that's all![29]
- Cabmen who *waited by the shutter*
- *Sweeping brooms*[30]

Chiana Valley is renowned for its prized breed of beef cattle known as the *Chianina* steak. Pirandello was fond of the area, vacationing in the small town of Chianciano Terme with his wife Antonietta and their three children. Lying between the towns of Montepulciano and Chiusi, Chianciano remains a famous hydrothermal resort. During a summer vacation there in 1905, Pirandello wrote two short stories, "Acqua Amara" ("Bitter Waters") and "Pallino e Mimì" ("Pallino and Mimì), which offer a vivid description of everyday life in the Tuscan village.

[28] Pirandello recorded this expression, which he heard in Montepulciano, using Tuscan spelling. He aimed at reproducing the Tuscan *gorgia* by way of the aspirated c, a phoneme typical of the Tuscan dialect.

[29] This exact phrase appears in the short story "La balia" ("The Wet Nurse"), published in 1903, the same year of Pirandello's Tuscan sojourn. Pirandello uses the phrase to describe the female protagonist Annicchia, an illiterate, uncouth southern girl who falls prey to a vicious man.

[30] Refers to the sound that straw brooms ("granate") make on the floor. The phrase appears in Pirandello's 1928 story, "Spunta un giorno" ("A Day Dawns"); its emotionally charged descriptions of sounds and illuminated objects function

- *Well woken-up!*
- Did the Mass *enter?* - It's *entering* now[31]
- If he takes the *trouble*[32] of leaving, that's fine; otherwise, nothing!
- In spite of his *shouting*, the opposite happens
- Front-facing rooms, 3 liras; back-facing, 2 liras
- Closed-fisted, punched him in his hip[33]
- To *pawn* something (at the Mount of Piety)[34]
- When he started something, he couldn't put an end to it! Always with the same reprimand!
- To buy on discount[35]

---

like a camera panning a scene. The shuffling of the brooms in the street, the first sound heard by the female protagonist upon recovering from an attempted suicide, suggests that life goes on regardless of human suffering.

[31] The verb *to enter* is here used to mean *start*. Though Pirandello was clearly struck by this usage, the expression is not found in any of his short stories or novels.

[32] In standard Italian, the word *accollo* means *burden*. In common parlance, it has a range of nuanced meanings, most of them involving an annoying person or situation. The Yiddish word *noodge* is a close equivalent. It is unsurprising that Pirandello uses the word in two short stories written after his stay in Montepulciano: "Sua Maestà" ("Her Majesty"), published in 1904, is set in a post-unified Sicily, where politicians are preoccupied with appearances over substance; and "La casa del Granella" ("Granella's House"), published in 1905, revolves around questions of moral responsibility.

[33] Closed-fisted punches are a recurring motif in Pirandello's short stories. They appear in criminal, religious, and marital contexts, as in (respectively) "La lega disciolta" ("The League Dissolved," 1910); "Il tabernacolo" ("The Shrine," 1903) and "L'avemaria di Bobbio" ("Bobbio's Hail Mary," 1912); and "Nenè e Ninì" ("Nenè and Ninì," 1912). As with other Tuscan expressions, Pirandello remembered the word long after his trip to Coazze.

[34] Pirandello is intrigued by the colloquial Tuscan expression "mettere in pegno," which means *to give something as a pledge*. He contrasts it with the institutional pawnbroking associated with the *mount of piety*, a charity that originated in the early Renaissance. The expression appears frequently in several of Pirandello's short stories, like "Volare" ("Flying," 1907) and "Il guardaroba dell'eloquenza" ("The Wardrobe of Eloquence," 1909). Even a decade after taking these notes, Pirandello continued to use the expression in his stories, as in "Visto che non piove" ("Since It's Not Raining," 1915). The recurrence of Tuscan words and phrases in his work reflects not just Pirandello's affinity for vernacular usages, but also his tendency to incorporate his notes into his fictional stories.

[35] The word "combinazione," signifying a deal or bargain, can be found in Pirandello's 1905 story "La morte addosso" ("Death Is Upon Him"), where it is used to describe secondhand furniture.

- Lying down belly up.[36]
- There you go! The button's gone!
- The small shop's wooden shutters
- Do you think I want to *wear my guts out* for you?[37]
- He starts getting fed up with it
- He didn't dress in black. As if he didn't feel the pain; as if he didn't care at all
- He didn't want to wait to take possession of it[38]
- In a frenzy to put it right, you can do worse
- To put prices on wares. How much? I'm not going to pay a lot for it. That's OK. We'll work it out.
- Sell wholesale
- You can't imagine how badly that breath stinks!
- With only a pair of arms ... What can I do?
- He thought he was losing his mind
- Is he asking me if I got hurt? Nothing ... I'm just almost dead.
- Son of a gun!
- And how the heck would I know that you were there!

---

[36] "A pancia all'aria" in the original Italian denotes the action of lying flat on your back "with your belly up," an otherwise idle position. A common Tuscan expression, it appears in many short stories Pirandello wrote soon after his 1903 summer in Montepulciano, e.g., "Pallino e Mimì" ("Pallino and Mimì"), "Fuoco alla paglia" ("Set Fire to the Straw"), "L'altro figlio" ("The Other Son"), "Va bene" ("It's Fine"), all published in 1905. The expression appears again in later tales, such as "Paura d'essere felice" ("Fear of Being Happy," 1911) and "Chi la paga" ("Who Pays the Piper," 1912). Throughout, the expression is used to characterize an idle protagonist.

[37] Another Tuscan colloquialism that Pirandello used frequently in his short stories. Connoting the feeling of being emotionally drained by someone else, the expression appears in several post-Montepulciano stories, such as "Di Guardia" ("Watch and Ward," 1905) and "Tra due ombre" ("Between Two Shadows," 1907), as well as in later stories, like "Fuga" ("Escape," 1912) and "Pena di vivere così" ("Such Is Life," 1920).

[38] In the 1904 story "Il fumo" ("The Fumes"), Pirandello built on the concept of "taking possession," referring to the Tuscan phrase he heard in Montepulciano. Focused on the harsh life of miners in Sicily's sulfur mines (a life he knew well from working in his father's mine as a young man), the story is full of Tuscan expressions, especially those from Montepulciano. This use of dialect reinforces the contrast between rural and industrial ways of life.

- Keep on walking (to get away quicker).
- Always clean-shaven, even when I'm sick — because I care.

- I don't understand, go figure!
- As quite as a mouse[39]
- Ohooo! - cried Don Filippino - Poor Tita.[40]
- Are you joking?[41]
- To let you vent
- Ah, I thought so! (I told you so! It seemed impossible to me)
- To rub the glass
- Imbecile! Aren't you ashamed to say such things?
- With two little hands you couldn't tell[42]
- The large red and black checkered handkerchief[43]
- "Cheep, cheep, cheep" (a way to call pigeons and doves)
- Eyes between the hair[44]

---

[39] Curiously, for this figure of speech, the original Italian mentioned a turtle.

[40] This exact line is used in the story "The Fumes." As the landlord Don Filippino dies, with his beloved monkey Tita watching, he worries who will take care of her.

[41] This particular version of the word "joke," *celia*, has fallen into disuse, though it can still be heard among older Florentine speakers. The word can be traced to a famous Florentine actress of the seventeenth century who amused audiences with her jokes. The word appears in the 1907 short story "La cassa riposta" ("The Replaced Casket"), which examines the double standards of shrewdness from the perspectives of an innkeeper and a miserly old lawyer.

[42] An exact reference to Donna Mimma's hands in the 1917 novella "Donna Mimma." Pirandello focuses on the Sicilian midwife's hands in the first section, when Donna Mimma is still highly esteemed in her village. In the second section, she is displaced by a younger midwife from the Piedmont region. Pirandello uses the Tuscan phrase not just to characterize Donna Mimma, but also to illustrate the differences between the midwives, as well as the cultural differences between north and south.

[43] The same handkerchief that Tino Labiso wears in "The Fumes": "the emblem of his unfortunate prudence."

[44] This colorful Tuscan expression refers to being woken up suddenly, or to someone who still seems to be sleeping. Although it piqued his interest, the expression isn't found anywhere in Pirandello's works.

- One of those girls who still wears a *bertuccia*[45]
- One says! (it is said!)
- Wanting to start a conversation no matter what
- A cowbell. To whom is the Holy Communion *given*? The Holy Communion is *passing by*.
- Eh, how would I know!? (Tell me about it!)
- Get up when it's still dark
- Push with the shoulder
- The milk puffs up first, then it boils
- A five-minute grace period
- It's not the right time: things don't work this morning,
- Come on, one kiss and it's all gone!
- To teach a class (in school)
- To go all around
- Imagine not seeing
- Hard-nosed (a stunned face)
- Tidbits
- Stuffing yourself – He stuffs his mouth as if he wanted to suffocate.
- He's a pain!
- She dropped the egg and it splashed on the floor
- *Chianna Chianna*, walking very slowly, like someone who'll never be on time
- Tweezing the first hair in your mustache
- He contorted his mouth, as though getting ready to tell his big secret

---

[45] In this context, a *bertuccia* is a ridiculous *hat*, following the Sienese definition. The word commonly means "monkey," used in a derogatory way to refer to a bland, ugly woman. Pirandello himself frequently used *bertuccia* in his stories to refer to unattractive female characters, as in "Donna Mimma," "Looking at a Print," "The Doctor's Duty," and "Far Away," the novel *The Old and the* Young, and the comedy *Man, Beast, and Virtue*. One notices his linguistic expertise when, for instance, he plays with the verb *sbertucciare* (derived from *bertuccia*), which means *to taunt*, but can also mean *to wear out*. Following his Tuscan retreat, Pirandello used *sbertucciati* (worn out) in stories such as "Lo scaldino" ("The Footwarmer") and "La scelta" ("The Choice"), both of whose protagonists struggle with the harsh realities of poverty.

- Do you want to go moldy?
- I can't stand beans

- To push someone
- Let's do at 1:00 pm
- To treat well
- 80% wine, more or less (judging by sight alone)
- Eyes brimming with tears
- I wouldn't dare try such a thing
- Nature never deprives anyone of what they need
- To attend to something – To pay attention to it
- *Roccia,* the dirt on the cheese crust[46]
- *Roccia,* the peel attached to the chestnut's brown husk
- When your fingers are *rocciose,* they are dirt-encrusted

ꟿ

Bookshelf[47]

ꟿ

- Carnations on the windowsill of a ruined house;[48] like the smile on a senile, toothless man recalling memories of youth

---

[46] The Tuscan word has been left untranslated to preserve its connotation, *dirt.* In standard Italian, *roccia* means *stone.* A fitting example of Pirandello's alternating use of the term *roccia* is the 1907 short story "Ciàula scopre la luna" ("Ciàula Discovers the Moon"). In it, a young miner finally discovers the beauty of the moon after spending all his nights underground in the sulfur mines. Pirandello used *roccia* to describe both the miners' rocky surroundings and Ciàula's dirty clothes. An alternate connotation of the word, referring to moldy cheese, appears in the 1910 story "La lega disciolta" ("The League Dissolved"), in which a filthy tablecloth is covered with *roccia.*

[47] Between the end of the Montepulciano notes and the beginning of the next set of notes, a section titled "Bookshelf" appears in the manuscript, showing a list of books Pirandello owned, or which he had a scholarly interest in. Missing in the Mondadori volume, this list has been included in this translation but moved at the end of the notes to maintain the narrative flow.

[48] Carnations often recur in Pirandello's creative writing as a symbol of regret and disillusion. In the 1895 short story "Il "no" di Anna" ("Lost and Found"), "dappled" carnations evoke the protagonist's grief over being ignored by the man she loves. In the 1916 one-act play "All'uscita" ("At the Exit"), the flowers represent

- The urge for things to crystallize into a given form.[49] Some ugly houses must always be like this – they can't be improved. Irritation. How mediocre certain lives are! How and why do they live like this?

ꙮ[50]

1909

JANUARY

"Sicilian Theater?" (*Rivista Popolare*)[51]	Liras 25.00
"Two Beds for Two" (*Marzocco*)[52]	" 30.00
"On the Italian Bosphorus" (*Marzocco*)[53]	" 25.00

---

the beauty of Nature that is often overlooked. And in the novel *Suo marito* (*Her Husband*), carnations adorn the table Giustino has set for his wife Silvia, but she ignores them, leaving her husband puzzled by her callousness.

[49] Throughout his career, Pirandello was obsessed with the disparity between human life and formality. For him, life was too intractable to be contained by social norms and obligations, a belief he held as early as 1901.

[50] What follows here is a list of incomes from both creative and scholarly work done in 1909. Judging by their number, it was a particularly prolific year. This section sheds light not only on Pirandello's increasing interest in theater, but also on his search for a language that could unify his art.

[51] The article "Teatro Siciliano?" ("Sicilian Theater?") appeared in the literary journal *Rivista Popolare di Politica, Lettere e Scienze sociali* on January 31, 1909. Founded in 1895 by Napoleone Colajanni, *Rivista Popolare* expressed social and political views which Pirandello shared with Colajanni. Among these was a concern with the *Fasci Siciliani*, a socialist movement in Sicily that emerged in the 1890s in opposition to unfair taxation and social discrimination. Pirandello invoked the Fasci in his 1913 novel *I vecchi e i giovani* (*The Old and the Young*) to illustrate the agrarian crisis in his native land. "Sicilian Theater?" demonstrates both his general interest in language and his support for Sicilian theater. Nevertheless, Pirandello questioned the feasibility of importing Sicilian plays to the peninsula.

[52] "Due letti a due" ("Two Double Beds"), a comic story published in *Il Marzocco* in 1909, was later included in the Bemporad collection, *La giara* (*The Jar*, 1928). The title mimics the symmetry of the tale's narrative structure. Divided into two scenes, the plot addresses death and grief from the perspectives of a widow and a widower who decide to get married. Their argument about who should be buried with whom (since both were previously married) eventually finds a comic and grotesque solution.

[53] "Sul Bosforo d'Italia" ("On the Italian Bosphorus") is an 1899 collection of short stories by the Sicilian poet and writer, Eduardo Giacomo Boner. Pirandello reviewed Boner's work in 1909, in a special issue of *Il Marzocco* on the devastating earthquake that destroyed Messina on December 28th, 1908. Boner died in the

"Among Chestnuts and Olive Trees" (*Nuova Antologia*)[54]	"	30.00
La Camminante (*Gazzetta del popolo*)[55]	"	20.00
Royalties from Treves[56]	"	36.45

---

earthquake. Pirandello was a keen admirer of Boner's *verismo* style, and even owned an autographed volume of his tales. He credited Boner with introducing German studies to Italy. In 1895, Pirandello dedicated to Boner ("with fraternal affection") his *Elegie renane* (*Rhenish Elegies*), a collection of poems influenced by the German Romantics. Two years later, Pirandello reviewed Boner's collection of nature poems, *La musa crociata* ("The Crusader Muse"), for the literary journal, *Roma letteraria* (July 10, 1897).

[54] A collection of nature poems published in 1909. The 30 liras reported here was more than Pirandello normally received for a short story, suggesting that he was paid for multiple submissions. Indeed, on January 16 of the same year, he submitted at least three poems to *Nuova Antologia*: "Pian della Britta," "Meriggio" ("Afternoon") and "A un olivo" ("To An Olive Tree"). These poems all celebrate the serenity of Soriano del Cimino, a small hill town nestled in the Cimini Mountains near Viterbo, in northern Lazio. Starting in 1907, Pirandello spent many of his summer breaks there with his family, always in search of inspiration. Some of his stories, such as 1911's "Canta l'epistola" ("Chants the Epistle") and 1913's "Rondone and Rondinello," are set there; it is also the subject of some of Pirandello's most iconic paintings and drawings. By all accounts, Pirandello enjoyed staying in picturesque Tuscia, and was sometimes joined by fellow intellectuals, such as Rosso di San Secondo and philologist Ernesto Monaci.

[55] Pirandello reviewed Giustino Lorenzo Ferri's novel *La camminante* (1908; *The Walker*) for *La Gazzetta del Popolo* on January 19th, 1909, praising its original narrative form and Ferri's deft handling of intimacy. In his essay "On Humor" (1908), Pirandello built on Ferri's aesthetic by describing the creative process in terms of an original vital force. As Pirandello saw it, Ferri's singular approach to fiction was not properly recognized by critics. The two writers were friends, sharing an interest in cinematography and moving in the same intellectual circles. They also co-founded the literary journal *Ariel* in 1895. As members of the so called "Bussi Gang," which gathered at the renowned Café Bussi in Rome on Via Veneto, Ferri and Pirandello hobnobbed with other literati such as Nino Martoglio, Lucio D'Ambra, and Luigi Capuana. For several years, Ferri substituted for Pirandello at the Istituto Superiore di Magistero, before the playwright left teaching for good in 1922 and devoted himself entirely to theater.

[56] While no letters exist documenting a personal relationship between Pirandello and the Treves family (as between Giovanni Verga and the Treves), their editorial partnership was indeed intense. In 1908, Treves printed a special edition of Pirandello's first full-length novel *The Outcast* (1893), which had been serialized in 1901 in the magazine *La tribuna*. The royalties Pirandello lists here are likely associated with the Treves printing, or perhaps with another collection of novellas, *Erma Bifronte* (*Two-faced Herm*), which Treves published in 1906. At any rate, Pirandello's frequent collaboration in these years with one of Italy's major publishing houses attests to his growing fame. In 1910, Treves printed a special edition of Pirandello's novel, *The Late Mattia Pascal*.

Salary		" 215.75
		382.20

FEBRUARY

Out of Tune (*Riviera Ligure*)[57]	Liras	25.00
"Presentation" (*La preparazione*)[58]	"	25.00
Wage increase	"	74.73
Wages	"	252.00
"Feminism" (*La preparazione*)[59]	"	25.00
		401.73

MARCH

Outstanding payments	Liras	370.00
Stipend	"	252.00
Appointment	"	92.50
		714.50

---

[57] Pirandello gathered three collections of poems, each published in *La Riviera Ligure* in 1904, 1905, and 1909, under the title *Fuori di chiave* (*Out of Tune*). The complete set appeared in 1912. The sum listed here might refer to an unidentified poem from the final collection. The title *Out of Tune* invokes a key point in Pirandello's aesthetics: the condition of being maladjusted to the world. In a 1905 review of Alberto Cantoni's novel *L'illustrissimo*, Pirandello described the sadness of this condition; a few years later, he made it a cornerstone of his essay, "On Humor" (1908). The evocative title was borrowed from an 1841 poem by Giuseppe Giusti, "Il ballo" ("The Ball"). See Alfredo Barbina, "Le *stonature* del Giusti e quelle di Pirandello," in "Ariel," XIII, 1-2, Jan-Aug 1998, pp. 59-61.

[58] "Presentazione" ("Presentation") is the first of three articles Pirandello wrote in February 1909. All were published under the title *Da lontano* in the triweekly politico-military journal, *La preparazione*, founded and directed by economist and sociologist Enrico Barone (1909-1915). Ostensibly a commentary on the times and a plea for strong leadership, Pirandello's essay—in the form of an interview with the imaginary philosopher and historian, Dr. Paulo Post—subtly analyzes misguided political thinking. Introduced here for the first time, Dr. Post returns in Pirandello's creative writing as Dr. Fileno, the protagonist of the 1911 short story, "La tragedia d'un personaggio" ("A Character's Tragedy"). Dr. Fileno's inverted perspective on reality is exemplary.

[59] The second article in the trio for *La preparazione*, "Feminismo" ("Feminism") was published on February 27-28, just two weeks after "Presentazione" ("Presentation"). In it, Pirandello addresses the question of women and labor only to disparage feminism as an "empty" conversation that history would sweep away. But this reactionary stance is at odds with his creative work, in which female characters often pursue intellectual professions. Among the most prominent examples is Silvia in the novel *Suo marito* (*Her Husband*), a character Pirandello modeled on the writer, Grazia Deledda, and whom he sketched out in his Coazze notes.

April

Article - *Preparazione*[60]	Liras	25.00
Stipend	"	344.30
		369.30

May

Novel - advance -		
Rassegna Contemporanea"[61]	Liras	250.00
Translation of *Le Courage Civique*[62]	"	15.00
Stipend	"	344.30
		609.30

June

Stipend and honorarium	Liras	599.60
End of first semester		3,086.63

---

[60] The unnamed article is likely the third and last essay in the trio, titled "Ricomincio a vedere l'Europa" ("I Start to See Europe Again"). Published in *La preparazione* on April 15-16, 1909, it features another interview with the fictional Dr. Post, this time on Italy's political and economic condition vis-à-vis Europe. Ironically, Dr. Post's recovery from a toothache is the pretext for regaining his wits. As in the first article, the conversation affords the reader an inverted perspective, following Dr. Post's principle of the "upside-down telescope."

[61] The unnamed "novel" likely refers to *I vecchi e i giovani* (*The Old and the Young*), which was serialized in 1909 in the literary journal *La rassegna contemporanea* and published in a single volume by Treves in 1913. In the intervening years, and particularly after his father-in-law's death in May 1909, Pirandello increased his submissions to journals and publishing houses. The period was one of considerable stress, as Antonietta's mental health became more unstable, and Pirandello had to confront ever-increasing expenses.

[62] In May 1909, Pirandello submitted an article to the *Revue politique et littéraire*, a French center-left political magazine nicknamed *Revue bleue* to distinguish it from *La Revue scientifique*, a pink-colored science magazine known as *Revue rose*. Émile Faguet, a renowned intellectual and literary critic for the *Revue bleue*, as well as a keen admirer of Pirandello, praised the writer's ironic treatment of courage. See Luigi Pirandello, « Le courage civique (Ironies de la vie et de la mort)», in "Revue politique et littéraire" (Revue bleue), tome I, 1909, pp. 362-365.

July

Stipend	Liras	345.30
Preparazione[63]	"	25.00
Marzocco - "In Defense of Mèola"[64]	"	30.00
		400.30

August

Stipend	Liras	345,30
Corriere della Sera[65]	"	250,00
		595,30

September

Rassegna Contemporanea[66]	Liras	250,00
Stipend	"	345,30
		595,30

October

From Treves for *Mattia Pascal*[67]	Liras	200,00
Stipend	"	300,00
		500.00

November

---

[63] This may be a reference to "Non conclude" (1909; "It Won't End"), an article Pirandello published in *La preparazione*. An almost-forgotten work, it prefigured the poetics of perception and self-construction at the heart of Pirandello's masterpiece, *Uno, nessuno e centomila* (*One, None, and a Hundred Thousand*). This novel's long gestation began in 1909 and wasn't published until 1926.

[64] Published in *Il Marzocco* on August 28, 1909, *Difesa del Mèola* is a satire on greed and narrow-mindedness in Italian society. The tale is part of a story collection titled *Tonache di Montelusa* (*Cassocks of Montelusa*).

[65] Pirandello wrote for *Corriere della sera* from 1909 until his death. In fact, his last submission was on December 8th, 1936, two days before he died. Pirandello submitted some of his most famous stories to the prestigious newspaper, such as "Mondo di carta: ("Paper World"), "La giara" ("The Jar"), "Ma non è una cosa seria" ("But It's Nothing Serious"), and "Pensaci Giacomino" ("Think It Over, Giacomino").

[66] See note 57.

[67] Treves published a special edition of *The Late Mattia Pascal* in 1910. The 200 liras recorded here might be an advance payment Pirandello received in light of his poor financial situation.

Honorarium	Liras	153.30
Corriere della Sera - "The Jar"[68]	"	100.00
Honorarium - supplement	"	8.00
Mattia Pascal - Balance[69]	"	164.00
Outstanding payments	"	359.60
Stipend	"	372.70
		1,157.60

DECEMBER

French translation - *Mattia Pascal*[70]	Liras	1,010.00
Short story - *Corriere*[71]	"	100.00
Stipend	"	372.70
		1,482.70
End of 2nd semester	Liras	4,731.20
Total for whole year:	Liras	3,086.63
		4,731.20
	Liras	7,817.80[72]

[68] "La giara" ("The Jar") was published in the *Corriere della sera* on October 20th, 1909, although Pirandello reported his payment for the story among his November earnings. One of his most popular stories, "La giara" illustrates the perils of coveting property, using a tyrannical Sicilian landowner as its villain. The story inspired a 1917 play by the same title and a popular 1924 ballet set to music by Alfredo Casella.

[69] A reference to Pirandello's payment in full for *The Late Mattia Pascal*, which Treves published in 1910. Although the novel was one of Pirandello's signal achievements, its publication coincided with a growing rift in his relationship with Treves. In 1909, at the same time he signed *Mattia Pascal*, Treves rejected another of Pirandello's manuscripts, *Her Husband*, because of the protagonist's striking resemblance to the Sardinian Nobel laureate Grazia Deledda.

[70] As Pirandello negotiated with Treves for the publication of *Mattia Pascal*, a French translation of the novel was being serialized in the *Journal de Genève* between July and September of 1909. At the end of that year, it was printed in book form by the Paris publisher, Calmann Lévy. The amount Pirandello records here is likely a royalty payment for this edition.

[71] Pirandello alludes here to the short story "Il lume dell'altra casa" ("The Light from the House Opposite"), which appeared in the *Corriere della sera* on December 12, 1909. The melodramatic tale, which revolves around adultery and the emotional toll it takes on a married woman, was later adapted into the first silent film that credited Pirandello. It was directed by Ugo Gracci in 1920.

[72] Pirandello's calculations are recorded incorrectly. His total earnings should be 7,817.83 liras.

1910[73]

JANUARY

Short story - *Corriere della sera*[74]	Liras	100.00
Stipend	"	372.70
		472.70

FEBRUARY

Short stories - *Corriere della sera*[75]	Liras	200.00
Carabba - "On Humor"[76]	"	74.60

---

[73] Only the first three months of 1910's earnings are reported. Nevertheless, we can see this was a very productive year for Pirandello, not only because of his many submissions but also because it marked the beginning of his career in theater. His first foray into playwriting was in 1898 with the short one-act play *L'epilogo* (*The Epilogue*), but it wasn't staged until 1910 under the new title *La morsa* (*The Vise*).

[74] In January 1910, Pirandello submitted not one but two short stories to the *Corriere della sera*: "Non è una cosa seria" ("It's Nothing Serious") and "L'uccello impagliato" ("The Stuffed Bird"). The first deals with marriage and adultery, and the second with the fear of death. Both exemplify the author's belief that reason and emotion are mutually irreconcilable. "It's Nothing Serious," which reworks the plot of another short story, "La signora Speranza" (1903; "Mrs. Hope"), was adapted for stage in 1918, in three acts, with the slightly altered title, *Ma non è una cosa seria* (*But It's Nothing Serious*). Although one of his least performed plays, the comedy was the source of two film adaptations, one directed by Augusto Camerini in 1920 and another by Mario Camerini in 1936.

[75] A reference to two short stories published in the *Corriere della sera*: "Benedizione" ("Blessings"), dated February 5th and "Pensaci Giacomino!" ("Think It Over, Giacomino!"), dated February 23rd. The more famous one was certainly the latter, which inspired the same-titled three-act play in Sicilian dialect, which Pirandello had tailored for Angelo Musco. The play was successfully staged in Rome in 1916. As this period coincides with Pirandello's commitment to regional theater, other Sicilian plays followed, such as *Liolà*, *Cap and Bells*, and *The Jar*, in spite of the controversy in early-twentieth-century Italy of staging plays in dialect. When *Think It Over, Giacomino!* was translated into standard Italian for the national stage and produced in 1920 by Ugo Piperino, it was not an immediate success. It would have to wait until Sergio Tofano's 1932 rendition for greater acclaim. In 1936, film director Gennaro Righelli turned *Think It Over, Giacomino!* into a successful film.

[76] A reference to the royalties from Pirandello's essay "On Humor," which Carabba published in 1908. Carabba was one of the most prestigious publishers in Abruzzo, active as early as 1892. Its editor Rocco Carabba published some of the most renowned intellectuals of the time, though he had a rocky relationship with

Stipend	"	372.70
		647.30

MARCH

Short story - *Corriere*[77]	Liras	100.00
Short story - *Natura e Arte*[78]	"	34.60
Stipend	"	372.70
		507.30

That timid child, CONFUSING
Still within me,
Woke up at sunrise
To be in church at daylight[79]

Pirandello, and the two had to go to court over a contractual violation. Pirandello had failed to fulfill his end of an agreement to write twelve short stories for a young readers series. Carabba rejected the first four stories as inappropriate and unoriginal, and Pirandello refused to write any more or to revise those he submitted. When Pirandello wrote down his earnings for 1910, the case was still pending and wouldn't be resolved until 1911, when Pirandello was ordered to pay 41 liras in damages.

[77] No evidence was found for a short story published in the *Corriere della sera* in March 1910. This might have been an error on Pirandello's part, perhaps confusing the publication date with an earlier or later submission. The fact that the 1901 report ends in March does not help considering how productive the following months were. Between April and November 1910, Pirandello submitted seven stories to the *Corriere* alone: "Il professor Terremoto" ("Professor Earthquake"), "Lo spirito maligno" ("Evil Spirit"), "La lega disciolta" ("The League Dissolved"), "La morta e la viva" ("The Living and the Dead"), "Leviamoci questo pensiero" ("Let's Get Rid of this Thought"), "Lo storno e l'angelo centuno" ("The Starling and the One Hundred and One Angel") (later renamed "Le maschere" ("The Masks"), and "Leonora Addio!" ("Farewell, Leonora!"). Some of these stories have not yet been translated into English; their English titles, therefore, are approximations.

[78] A reference to the short story "Musica vecchia" ("Old Music"), which was published on February 1, 1910 in *Natura e Arte,* a bimonthly illustrated journal active from 1891 to 1911. Focused on the arts and sciences, *Natura e Arte* published the work of major Italian intellectuals. Pirandello himself submitted a wide range of pieces, from fiction and poetry to essays and reviews, and took part in debates organized by the journal.

[79] In the manuscript, this stanza is written upside down on the notebook's last page. It is displayed here in the same place as in the Mondadori edition to preserve readability and continuity.

ꕥ

The paternal thief[80]

Oh, my Lord Jesus Christ

ꕥ[81]

1904[82]

Wages		£ 2,592.00
January 2nd	*Riviera Ligure*	
("The Husband's Revenge")[83]		£ 25.00
January 16th		
Nuova Antologia (Literary News)[84]		£ 64.00
January 19th *Marzocco*[85]		£ 100.00

[80] This enigmatic phrase, which precedes the invocation to Christ, might refer to an expression Pirandello heard. It could also be an original construction he intended to rework in his writing.

[81] At this point in the manuscript, Pirandello records expenses from 1905, e.g., cigarettes, newspapers, tickets, coffee. Given its limited relevance, the brief list was omitted from this translation, following the Mondadori reference volume.

[82] Unlike the 1909 and 1910 reports, Pirandello's 1904 list of incomes is precise. He not only includes dates, but also specifies the titles of work he was paid for.

[83] Published in *La Riviera Ligure*, the story "La buon'anima" ("The Dearly Departed," 1904) is about the tricks the dead play on the living. It was republished in 1910 by Treves along with a set of other novellas, collectively titled *La vita nuda* (*The Naked Life*).

[84] The "literary news" refers to Pirandello's long and detailed review of Giuseppe Aurelio Costanzo's 1903 lyrical poem "Dante." Almost completely forgotten today, Costanzo was a skillful poet known for his experimental verse and his nostalgic perspective, which Pirandello was careful to recognize. It is perhaps unsurprising that a poem like "Dante," with its juxtaposition of tradition and new poetic trends, was reviewed in a journal such as *Nuova Antologia*. Founded in 1866 in Florence by Francesco Protonotari, the journal sought to preserve the vision of the previous *Antologia* directed by Gino Capponi and Gian Pietro Vieusseux (1821-1833). Today, *Nuova Antologia* is regarded as one of Europe's oldest and most prestigious literary journals. Pirandello was a prolific contributor of both fiction and reviews, from as early as 1902, with the publication of the novella "Lontano" ("Far Away"), until his death.

[85] Pirandello's career was intertwined with *Il Marzocco*, a literary journal founded in Florence in 1866 by Adolfo and Angiolo Orvieto. At Gabriele D'Annunzio's suggestion, the journal was named after the copper heraldic lion of the Florentine Republic. Elegant in its engraving and typography, *Il Marzocco* stood in the vanguard

January 23rd Ministry	£	1,202.00
February 1st Supplementary honorarium	£	12.20
February 14th *Marzocco* - ("Into the Sketch")[86]	£	25.00
March 18th *Jugend* - (Tr. "Sunrise")[87]	£	61.66
May 2nd *Marzocco* ("The Vigil")[88]	£	30.00
July 3rd *Marzocco* (S.M.)[89]	£	30.00

---

of the new aesthetic movement, fostering D'Annunzio's predilection for Symbolist art. Not until 1900, under Adolfo Orvieto, did the journal radically shift its focus from belles-lettres to a celebration of Florence's historical and cultural tradition. Pirandello continued submitting his work, including "Prima notte" ("Wedding Night"), his novella "Lumie di Sicilia" ("Sicilian Limes"), his collection of poems, *Zampogna* (*Bagpipes*, written between 1892 and 1898), and his short story "Nel segno" (1904; "Into the Sketch"), for which he was paid the 25 liras reported in the *Notebook*. Nevertheless, Pirandello's output dropped, partly because he needed to pursue more lucrative assignments after his 1903 financial crisis, and because of the journal's shifting trends. In the following years, *Il Marzocco* became more hostile to what it called "decorative literature," and from 1911 to 1914, published mainly propaganda in support of Italian revival. With the outbreak of World War I, the journal was increasingly politicized, going so far as to support D'Annunzio's imperialistic League of Fiume. *Il Marzocco* stopped publishing in 1932.

[86] Originally published in *Il Marzocco*, "Nel segno" ("Into the Sketch," 1904) was later included in the story collection *La vita nuda* (*Naked Life*), issued in 1922 by the Florentine publisher, Bemporad. On May 27, 1913, Pirandello wrote to Nino Martoglio, a respected screenwriter for the production company, *Cines*, offering "Into the Sketch" as a potential script; he described the story as "very beautiful - almost ready," and requested an immediate advance of 500 liras, reflecting Pirandello's pursuit of windfall profits and a stroke of luck in the nascent film industry. See *Pirandello-Martoglio carteggio inedito*, ed. Sarah Zappulla-Muscarà, Milan: Pan Editrice, 1979, p. 19.

[87] In March 1909, a translation of Pirandello's short story "Levata del sole" ("Sunrise") was published in the distinguished German journal, *Jugend*. Founded in Munich by George Hirth in 1896, *Jugend* was dedicated to literature and the arts, and featured rich illustrations. News of the publication, which was translated by Nini Knoblich, was proudly reported in the March issue of *Nuova Antologia*, in a special section devoted to "Italians Abroad."

[88] The story "La veglia" ("The Vigil") explores the issue of forgiveness as a husband stands vigil beside his dying adulterous wife. Pirandello incorporated the scene into his three-act play *Come prima, meglio di prima* (*As Before, Better Than Before*, 1919) about a fallen woman who pretends to be her husband's second wife. As true mother and false stepmother, she becomes estranged from real self, and has to escape in order to survive.

[89] The abbreviation S.M. stands for "Sua Maestà" ("Her Majesty"), the title of Pirandello's 1904 short story published in *l Marzocco* on July 3. A comic sequel to a previous tale, "L'imbecille" ("The Imbecile"), "Her Majesty" is set during the post-unification struggle for political power, and exposes the equivocation among politicians and their infighting, which took precedence over the common

May/June *Nuova Antologia* (*Late Mattia Pascal*)[90]	£	906.00
July 3rd Honorarium Exams	£	245.65
July 18th Exam Commissioner in Alatri[91]	£	350.00
August 21st *Marzocco* ("The Medals")[92]	£	30.00
August 26th *Riviera Ligure* ("The Cathar Heresy")[93]	£	25.00
October 12th *Marzocco* ("The Fly")[94]	£	30.00

---

good. In 1915, "Her Majesty" was reprinted under the title "Erba del nostro orto" ("The Grass in Our Garden").

[90] Pirandello's great novel was serialized bimonthly by *Nuova Antologia*, from April 16 to June 16, 1904. The income Pirandello lists here was the last in a period of financial insecurity, worsened by the flooding of the family sulfur mine. The book's success was restorative, allowing Pirandello to continue pursuing his career as a writer.

[91] In the summer of 1904, Pirandello accepted an appointment as exam commissioner after Giovanni Pascoli rejected the offer. Limited financial resources forced Pirandello to take any job, though he never lost hope of making a living as an artist. According to legend, while in Alatri, Pirandello worked feverishly on his novel *The Late Mattia Pascal* during exam session breaks. Despite the drudgery of the work, Pirandello found relief from the stresses of family life and was able to write in his spare time. His fond memories of Alatri resurface in the 1911 story "O di uno o di nessuno" ("Either of One or of No One"), which is partially set in the central Italian hill town.

[92] Published in 1904, the short story "Le medaglie" ("The Medals") indirectly expresses Pirandello's attitude about Garibaldi's heroic unification campaign – a topic also central to *The Old and the Young* (1913). If the novel deflates the Risorgimento's idealism, then "The Medals" downplays Italy's national myth by emphasizing the nationalists' rhetorical dishonesty; for Pirandello, nationalism and political disenchantment go hand in hand. To drive the point home, the story's protagonist is unmasked while wearing the medals his brother had won for merit in Garibaldi's Expedition of the Thousand.

[93] Although listed among his 1904 earnings, Pirandello's short story "L'eresia catara" ("The Cathar Heresy") is believed to have been printed in *La Riviera Ligure* in February 1905. The tale was republished the following year in *Erma Bifronte* (*Two-faced Herm*) with a dedication to Luigi Capuana. One of his least known tales, "The Cathar Heresy" is a critique of phony intellectualism, which regarded contemporary national literature as inferior to foreign works. The title refers to a heretical medieval Christian sect and its pursuit of spiritual purity.

[94] Written shortly after his Coazze retreat, "La mosca" ("The Fly") explores human identity from the grim perspective of a fly. The insect is both a symbol of nature's indifference to human suffering and, crucially, an agent of fate: it mortally infects the two main characters and ruins their plan of getting married. To Pirandello, nature is an inexorable force that shapes human life and fortune. This attitude is also expressed in the conclusion of *Her Husband*, when Silvia returns from her solitary retreat in Coazze having abandoned herself to the natural world.

October 13th Exam commissioner (Alatri)	£	244.50
October 13th German translation of "Il vitalizio"[95]	£	45.75
November 16th *Zampogna* (one copy)[96]	£	1.25
November 18th Honorarium admission exams	£	103.60
December 6th *Regina*[97]	£	50.00
December 16th *Marzocco* "La fedeltà del cane" ("Man's Best Friend")[98]	£	30.00
	£	6,203.61

---

[95] 1904 officially marks the beginning of Pirandello's international celebrity. Besides the publicized translations into French and German of *The Late Mattia Pascal,* Pirandello announced the publication of a second short story in German, "Il vitalizio" ("The Annuity"). Written in 1901, the story pokes fun at the arrogance of those who think they can fool Death. Where "The Annuity" was published is unknown.

[96] A collection of poems originally published in 1901, *Zampogna* (*Bagpipes*) was Pirandello's fourth collection after *Mal giocondo* (*Playful Evil,* 1899), *Elegie Renane* (*Rhenish Elegies,* 1895), and *Pasqua di Gea* (*Easter of Gea,* 1891). It marks the beginning of a symbolist period in Pirandello's poetry, having shaken off the influence of Carducci. In this "raccolta di rime agresti" ("collection of rustic rhymes"), as Pirandello called them, the treatment of nature and human emotions bears a new influence: that of Pascoli. To many critics, *Bagpipes* anticipates the poetic experimentalism of 1912's *Fuori di chiave* (*Out of Tune*), Pirandello's final collection of lyric poems.

[97] "Una voce" ("A Voice") was first published in the periodical *Regina* on September 20, 1904. It was included in *Erma bifronte* (*Two-faced Herm*) in 1906. It is unclear why Pirandello listed the story with his December earnings, or why he earned 50 liras, which is double the amount he received on average for a single piece. "A Voice" tells the story of a blind nobleman who falls in love with his deceased mother's servant. In a hopeless attempt to keep his feelings alive, the servant conceals the fact that his blindness is curable. It is worth noting that the story first appeared in the newly founded Neapolitan journal *Regina* (1904—1920), a publication for women about art, culture, and fashion. Directed by Carlo Crocco Egineta, *Regina* featured a portrait of a famous woman on every cover as part of a campaign for female emancipation. Among its most zealous contributors were Pascoli, D'Annunzio, Antonio Beltramelli, and Salvatore Di Giacomo. As far as we know, "A Voice" is the only short story Pirandello submitted to the journal.

[98] Published in *Il Marzocco*" in December 1904, "La fedeltà del cane" ("Man's Best Friend") addresses the themes of adultery, disillusion, and betrayal by showing the ways in which animals are superior to men.

ထ

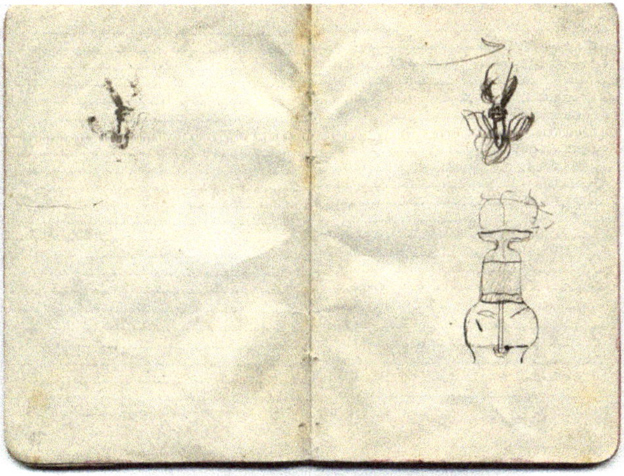

Drawing of a lamp and a candle[99]

[99] In the original manuscript, two sets of drawings are separated by figures and calculations. Since they lack significance, the numbers have been omitted from this translation, just as they were from the Mondadori.

Two drawings (portrait and a clown)[100]

[100] The drawings of a human head and a jester are followed, on the last page of the notebook, by four stanzas written upside down. These have been moved to the front and re-oriented, following the Mondadori edition. The beginning of a recipe appears after the short lyric. It reads: "One egg, one small spoon of flour and two of sugar." It is unclear what this is a recipe for.

List of Books

Bookshelf[101]

1. Pellegrini *Elementi di Letteratura*
2. Pellissier *Movimenti Cont. della Lett. Francese* (Romagnoli)
3. Tommaseo *L'Educazione del Giovane Italiano*
4. Mestica *Istituzioni di Letteratura* (2 vol.)
5. Denis *La Comédie greque* (2 vol.)
6. Rajna *Le fonti dell'O.F.*
7. Graf *Studi drammatici*
8. Del Lungo *Dal secolo e dal Poema di Dante*
9. Barzellotti *I. Taine*
10. Mazzoni *Tra libri e carte*
11. Carollo *Studio Dantesco*
12. Chiarini *G. Carducci - Impressioni e ricordi*
13. Costetti *Il teatro it. nel 1800*
14. Flamini *Studii di St. Lett.*
15. Vannucci *Studi Storici e Morali sulla Lett. Latina*
16. Scartazzini *Dante Prolegomeni*
17. De Sanctis *G. Leopardi*

---

[101] Originally titled *Libreria* in the manuscript, this list is composed of books that were of interest to Pirandello at the time he was writing down his thoughts in the *Notebook*. For the most part, all these books can still be found in his private studio in the house on Via Antonio Bosio in Rome, the playwright's last residence and now the headquarters of the *Istituto di Studi Pirandelliani*. The list sheds light on Pirandello's interest in contemporary criticism (De Sanctis, Rajna, Capuana, Carducci) as well as in conceptualizing the idea of humor, which led to the publication of his seminal essay *On Humor* in 1908. The two volumes on the history of literary criticism by Alessandro d'Ancona engaged Pirandello's interest in Cecco Angiolieri, a 13th century Italian poet considered the master of comic verse. Pirandello reviewed D'Ancona's study of Angiolieri in 1886, and this became the starting point for his theory on humor. In the years to come, D'Ancona's analysis prevented Pirandello from labeling any medieval poet a "humorist."

18. D'Ancona *Studi di Lett. It.*
19. D'Ancona *Studi di Critica*
20. Torraca *Saggi e Rassegne*
21. Canello *Saggi di crit. lett.*
22. Carducci *Confessioni e Battaglie* (2 vol.)
23. Imb. *Studi Danteschi*
24. Marc Monnier *Renaissance*
25. Carducci *Conversazioni critiche*
26. Trezza *Studii critici*
27. Morandi *Antologia critica*
28. Bartoli *Commedia dell'arte*
29. Sudby *Brunetto Latini*
30. Pitrè *Feste patronali in Sicilia*
31. Capuana *Gl'ismi contemporanei*
32. Voigt *Risorgimento dell'antichità classica* (2 vol)
33. Nyrop *Epopea francese*
34. Canello *A. Daniello*
35. Zannoni *I precursori di Merlin Cocai*
36. Rajna *Le corti d'amore*
37. Mahly *A. Poliziano*

The Missing Page

Found in 2001 in the archives of Houghton Library at Harvard University by Italian scholar Ombretta Frau, the missing page is believed to be page 3 (recto and verso) of the manuscript, as suggested by the similarities in content with the previous pages.

Indeed, Pirandello's description of the gloomy gorges and foaming waterfall mirrors the notes he dated Sunday, August 25th, in which he contrasted the solemnity of nature to the cheerfulness of the valley. The same mountain scenery will serve as background for the short story "Di guardia ("Watch and Ward," 1905).

Absent from both the Mondadori and the 2000 Agrigento editions, the missing page is reproduced here in the original Italian with permission of Houghton Library at Harvard, where the manuscript is held [MS Ital 83.2. Houghton Library, Harvard University].

RIGHT PAGE[102]

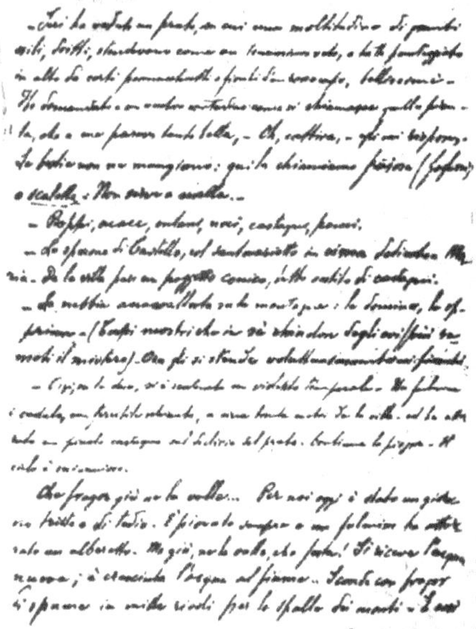

[102] *Transcription*: [Ieri ho veduto un prato su cui una moltitudine di gambi esili, dritti, stendevano come un tenuissimo velo, e tutto punteggiato in alto da certi pennacchietti o fiocchi d'un rosso cupo, bellissimi.

Ho domandato a un Vecchio contadino come si chiamasse quella pianta, che a me pareva tanto bella, - Oh, cattiva, - egli mi rispose, - Le bestie non ne mangiano: qui la chiamano früiosa (fogliosa) o *scaletta*. Non serve a nulla.

- Pioppi, acacie, ontani, noci, castagni, pomi.
- Lo sperone del Castello, col santuarietto in cima a Maria. Da la villa pare un poggetto conico, tutto vestito di castagni.
- La nebbia accavallata su le montagne: le domina, le opprime. (Cupi mostri che in sé stridon degli evi/ più remoti il mistero). Ora gli si stende voluttuosamente sui fianchi.
- Oggi, su le due, si è scatenato un violento temporale. Un fulmine è caduto, un terribile schianto, a circa trenta metri da la villa - ed ha atterrato un piccolo castagno sul declivio del prato - Continua la pioggia - Il cielo è minaccioso.

Che fragor giù nella valle ... Per noi oggi è stato un giorno triste e di tedio. È piovuto sempre e un fulmine ha atterrato un alberetto. Ma giù, ne la valle, che festa! Si riceve l'acqua nuova; è cresciuta l'acqua al fiume ... scende con fragor di spume in mille rivoli per le spalle dei monti. È così ...]

Yesterday I saw a lawn with a multitude of slender, erect stems spread like an evanescent veil, all dotted on top with dark red hackles or flakes - wonderful.[103]

I asked an old farmer for the name of that flower which looked so beautiful to me. "Oh, terrible" - he replied - "Not even beasts eat it. Here we call it früiosa (leafy) or *scaletta*. It's good for nothing."[104]

- Poplars, acacia trees, alders, walnut trees, chestnut trees, pomes.
- The castle, situated on an outcrop, with its little sanctuary dedicated to the Virgin Mary. From the villa, it looks like a conical knoll, covered up by chestnut trees.[105]
- The fog piles up on the mountains: it dominates them, it oppresses them. (Gloomy monsters squeaking /the mystery of the oldest ages. Now the fog voluptuously wraps around their sides.
- Today, around 2 pm, a raging storm. A flash of lightning, a terrible roar, about thirty meters from the villa - it struck a little chestnut tree on the meadow's slope. It keeps raining - the sky is threatening.

What a noise down in the valley ... For us the day was sad and tedious.[106] It rained all the time and a bolt of

---

[103] The same exact scenery and the "dark red hackles" are faithfully re-used in the short story "Watch and Ward."

[104] In "Watch and Ward," this exchange is reproduced almost verbatim, though in the story it is between the Generalessa and Mr. Raspi. Pirandello infused his own wonder into the simple-minded Generalessa, who is reprimanded by Mr. Raspi for being fooled so easily by the flowers' entrancing color and ignoring their poisonous nature. Pirandello here uses his notes to add humor to his narration, thus anticipating his future poetics and interest in the discrepancy between appearance and emotion.

[105] Nowadays, "Pirandello's trail," as locals call it, leads away from the center of Coazze to a castle on a hill. Pirandello's note suggests a view from the trail. The sanctuary he refers to is still standing, together with the lighthouse built in 1961 to celebrate the 100th anniversary of Italy's unification.

[106] A very rare instance in the *Notebook* of Pirandello hinting at the other family members accompanying him in Coazze. Typically, his notes are limited to very personal insights and observations on the surroundings and the local residents.

lightning struck down a tree. But down in the valley, what a feast! There's fresh water; the river flows higher ... It runs down loud and foamy into a thousand streams through the rear mountains.[107] The Sangone ...

[107] These descriptions recall previous ones, thus supporting the theory that the missing page found in the Harvard archive is indeed page 3.

LEFT PAGE[108]

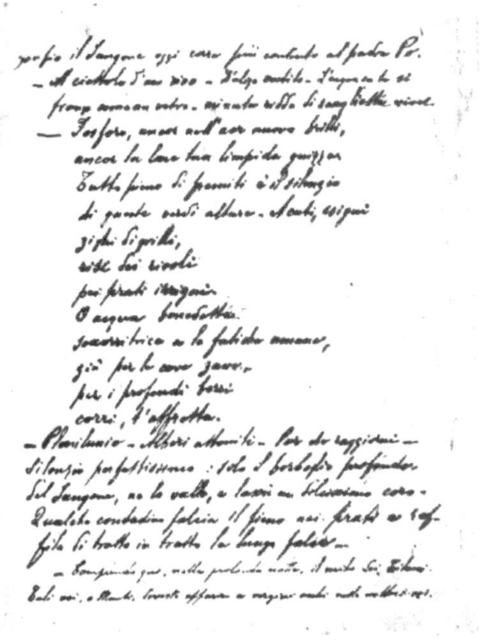

---

[108] Transcription [... gonfio il Sangone oggi corre più contento al padre Po.

- Al ciottolo d'un rivo - D'aliga vestito - L'acqua su te si frange come un vetro - minuta ridda di scagliette vive.

_______ Fosforo, ancor nell'aer nuovo brilli,
ancor la luce tua limpida guizza.

Tutto pieno di fremiti è il silenzio
di queste verdi alture. Acuti, esigui
zighi di grilli,
risi dei rivoli
per prati irrigui.
O acqua benedetta
soccorritrice a le fatiche umane,
giù per le cave zane,
per i profondi borri
corri, t'affretta.

- Plenilunio - Alberi attoniti - Par che raggiorni - Silenzio perfettissimo: solo il borboglio profondo del Sangone, ne la vale, e lassù un dolcissimo coro. Qualche contadino falcia nei prati e raffila di tratto in tratto la lunga falce ...
- Comprendo qui, nella profonda notte, il mito dei Titani. Tali voi, o monti, doveste apparire a vergini occhi nella notte, voi ...]

... is overflowing today and runs happily into father Po.[109]

- To the river pebble - adorned with algae - The water breaks against you like glass - a small clot of lively flakes.[110]

_____ Phosphorus, you still shine in the new air,
Your clean light still flickers.
All filled with trembling is the silence
Of these green hills. Sharp, minute
Chirping of crickets,
Laughing streams,
Through the wet meadows.[111]
Oh, blessed water,
Reward for human labor,
Down the hollow gorges,
Though the deep gullies,
You run hastily.[112]

- Full moon - astonished trees - it seems as if it's dawning - perfectly silent; only the deep mumbling of the Sangone River down in the valley and a sweet chorus up there.[113] Some farmers mow the hay in the meadows and occasionally sharpen the long sickle ...

---

[109] The Po (the longest Italian river) is here personified as the "father" of all other rivers. Its stature is contrasted with the smaller Sangone, a local river.

[110] These four verses would later be reworked in Pirandello's short story "Watch and Guard," in which the water still crashes against a river pebble "adorned with algae."

[111] These verses would later appear in the second stanza of the poem "Cargiore," published in *La Riviera Ligure* in 1903. The poem can be traced to Pirandello's sustained contemplation of the scenery in Coazze. The last stanza also reworks the image of the farmers mowing the hay and sharpening their sickles, as recorded in the notes on the missing page.

[112] The hymn to "phosphorus" and the salutary effect of water on the meadows expand on the imagery of the previous pages and appear in the short stories "Youth" and "Watch and Guard." A "beneficial rain" returns also in the *Taccuino di Harvard* (c. 32r), demonstrating how Pirandello consistently drew inspiration from his notes, sometimes even cross-referencing them to create narrative patterns.

[113] One of the most evocative and recurring tropes in Pirandello's work, the moon is often symbolic of primitive, untainted emotion. It prompts an identification with nature and a rejection of absolute truth. In these notes, the moon seems to preside over the harmony of natural elements.

- Here, in deepest night, I understand the Titans' myth.[114] And so should you, oh Mountains, appear to virgin eyes in the night, you ...

[114] Pirandello was drawn to mythology for its celebration of eternal values and promotion of collective identity. Seeking to capture "the primitive and natural forces of the spirit" - as he often professed - he also considered myth a counter-force to reality, as well as a means of understanding modernity. His famous theater trilogy, produced in the torturous last phase of his career, uses mythological archetypes as metaphors to clarify the problems posed by the modern age. One can see this in *The New Colony* (*La nuova colonia*, 1926), which ponders the unsuccessful attempt to transform a deserted island into a just and egalitarian society, and in *Lazarus* (*Lazzaro*, 1928), where the fusion of man with nature is effected by a religious symbolism inspired by the author's pantheism. However, it was not until *The Mountain Giants* (*I giganti della montagna*, 1937), the only unfinished play in the trilogy, that Pirandello explored the role of art in modern society against the prevailing materialism.

Bibliography

Alessio, Antonio. *Pirandello pittore.* Agrigento: Ed. del Centro Naz. di Studi Pirandelliani, 1984.

_______. *I Pirandello ritornano al Caos: la pittura passione artistica della famiglia.* Agrigento: Biblioteca-Museo Luigi Pirandello, 2003.

Alvaro, Corrado. *Scritti su Pirandello.* Soveria Mannelli: Rubbettino, 2013.

Andreoli, Annamaria. *Taccuino segreto.* Milano: Mondadori, 1997.

Andreoli, Annamaria (ed). *I libri in maschera. Luigi Pirandello e le biblioteche.* Roma: De Luca, 1996.

Barbina, Alfredo. *La biblioteca di Luigi Pirandello.* Roma: Bulzoni, 1980.

Bono, Michele. "Nel laboratorio di Pirandello: Il ruolo dei *Taccuini* nella costruzione di *Suo marito.*" In *Aevum,* Anno 88, Fasc. 3 (Settembre-Dicembre 2014): 729-744.

Bussino, Giovanni. "Il fecondo soggiorno di Pirandello a Coazze." In *Canadian Journal of Italian Studies,* Vol.6 (22): 1983.

Casella, Paola. *L'Umorismo di Pirandello: ragioni intra e intertestuali.* Firenze: Cadmo, 2002.

Dell'Orto, Giovanni. *Sui monti di Coazze.* Coazze: Busca L.C.L., 1983.

De Luca, Liana. "Il Taccuino di Coazze." In *Vernice. Rivista di formazione e cultura.* Anno XIII, n. 35: pp. 103-116.

Dolfi, Anna, Nicola Turi, and Rodolfo Sacchettini (eds.). *Memorie, autobiografie e diari nella letteratura italiana dell'Ottocento e del Novecento.* Pisa: ETS, 2008.

Frau, Ombretta. *Da Girgenti a Coazze: percorsi letterari nei taccuini di Luigi Pirandello.* Thesis. Harvard University Archives, 2002.

_______. "La tessera mancante del *Taccuino di Coazze.*" In *Pirandello e il Piemonte. Atti del convegno internazionale di studi.* Torino: Enterprise GFS comunicazione, 2004. 38-44.

Frau, Ombretta and Cristina Gragnani (eds.). *Taccuino di Harvard.* Milano: Mondadori, 2002.

Garosi, Linda. "I Taccuini di Pirandello, ovvero l'immaginario fantastico nella stanza segreta dello scrittore." In *Forum Italicum,* Vol.52 (3), 2018: 745-762.

Gaudenzio, Claretta. *Di Giaveno, Coazze e Valgioie: cenni storici con annotazioni e documenti inediti.* Savigliano: L'artistica, 1988.

Gieri, Manuela. *Contemporary Italian Filmmaking: Strategies of Subversion; Pirandello, Fellini, Scola, and the Directors of the New Generation.* Toronto: University of Toronto Press, 1995.

Gioanola, Elio. *Pirandello's story: la vita o si vive o si scrive.* Milano: Jaka Book, 2007.

Guglielminetti, Marziano. *Dalla parte dell'io: modi e forme della scrittura autobiografica nel Novecento.* Napoli: Edizioni Scientifiche Italiane, 2020.

_______. *Il romanzo del Novecento italiano: strutture e sintassi.* Roma: Editori Riuniti, 1986.

Lo Vecchio Musti, Manlio (ed.). Luigi Pirandello. *Il taccuino di Coazze.* In *Saggi, poesie, scritti varii.* Milano: Mondadori, 1960. 1237-1246.

Lugnani, Lucio. "Vecchi taccuini e nuovi pirandellisti." In *Ariel,* n. 1 and 2, Gen/Ago. 1998.

Marsili, Renata Antonetti. *Lina e Luigi Pirandello: una vita straordinaria.* Milano: Azimut, 2007.

Marsili, Renata Antonetti, Fabio Pierangeli, Silvia Nicoletta Tesè, Andrea Gareffi (eds.). *Luigi Pirandello: biografia per immagini.* Torino: Gribaudo, 2001.

_______. *Luigi Pirandello intimo. Lettere e documenti inediti.* Roma: Gangemi, 1998.

Milaneschi, Cesare. *Una storia "a suo modo": la Chiesa Valdese di Coazze.* Cosenza: Editoriale Progetto 2003.

Nardi, Florinda. *L'emozione feconda. Luigi Pirandello e la creazione artistica.* Roma: Nuova Cultura, 2008.

Occhipinti, Emanuele. *Travelling In and Out of Italy. 19th and 20th-Century Notebooks, Letters and Essays.* Cambridge Scholars Pub., 2011.

O'Rawe, Catherine. *Authorial Echoes. Textuality and Self-plagiarism in the Narrative of Luigi Pirandello.* Taylor & Francis, 2017.

Pierangeli, Fabio. *Una "luce particolare, non so come descriverla ..." Città, luoghi, viaggi della letteratura contemporanea.* Roma: Edizioni Nuova Cultura, 2006.

Sarti, Lisa and Michael Subialka (eds.). *Pirandello's Visual Philosophy. Imagination and Thought Across Media.* Madison, NJ: Fairleigh Dickinson UP, 2017.

Sarti Lisa and Michael Subialka (eds.). Luigi Pirandello, *Stories for a Year.* Digital Edition, www.pirandellointrans lation.org, 2021.

Sarti, Lisa, Michael Subialka, Carlo Di Lieto. *Scrittura d'immagini.Pirandello e la visualità tra arte, filosofia e psicoanalisi.* Soveria Mannelli: Rubbettino, 2021.

Squarzina, Luigi. *"Ciascuno a suo modo" di Pirandello e il teatro totale delle Avanguardie.* Roma: Bulzoni, 1987.

Zangrilli, Franco. *L'arte novellistica di Pirandello.* Ravenna: Longo, 1983.

"Acqua Amara" ("Bitter Waters") 20, 39n27
Agrigento viii, x, xi, xiii, xiv, xv, 1n1, 5, 6, 10, 61, 69
Alatri 23, 55, 55n91, 56,
"All'uscita" ("At the Exit") 44n48,
Almanacco Letterario Bompiani 5
Alps vii, 1, 9, 14, 23, 26, 34n13, 35n14, 38n27,
Alvaro, Corrado 5, 23n7
Andreoli, Annamaria 23n7
Anticoli Corrado 23
Ariel 46n55, 47n57, 70

Balangero 36
Barone, Enrico 47n58
Basilica of Superga 36n18
Beffe della morte e della vita (*Jests of Life and Death*) 16, 37n20
Bell tower xivn3, 2, 16, 16n6, 17, 18, 29, 30n3,
Beltramelli 56n97
"Benedizione" ("Blessings") 51n75
Biblioteca-Museo Luigi Pirandello viii, xi, xii, xivn3, 1n1, 5
Bocciarda (Mount) 36
Boner, Eduardo Giacomo 45n53
Brando 36
Brunello 36

Camerini, Mario 51n74
"Canta l'epistola" ("Chants the Epistle") 46n54
Cantoni, Alberto 47n57
Capobianco, Filomena 1n1, 2n3, 5
Capuana, Luigi 46n55, 55n93, 59, 60, 77
Carabba, Rocco 51, 51n76,
Carducci, Giosuè 30n6, 38n26, 56n96, 59, 60, 73
Cargiore 36, 37n23, 66n111
Casale Inverso 35
Casella, Alfredo 50n68
Cecè (*Cecè*) 8
"Chi la paga" ("Who Pays the Piper") 41n36
Chiana Valley 38, 38n27,
Chianciano 39n27
Chiusi 38, 39n27
Ciascuno a suo modo (*Each in His Own Way*) 2, 16, 16n6, 17, 30n3, 78
"Ciàula scopre la luna" ("Ciàula Discovers the Moon") 44n46
Cimini Mountains 46n54
Cines 54n36
Coazze
Colajanni, Napoleone 45n51
Colle di Braida 33, 34, 34n13
Come prima, meglio di prima (*As Before, Better Than Before*) 54n38
Corriere della Sera 49, 49n65, 50, 50n68, 50n71, 51, 52
Costa del Pagliaio 36
Costanzo, Giuseppe Aurelio 53n84
Cottian Alps 9, 29n2, 35n15,
Crocco Egineta, Carlo 56n97
Cugno dell'Alpet 36

"Dal naso al cielo" ("From Nose to Sky") 14
D'Ambra, Lucio 5, 46n55
D'Annunzio, Gabriele 53n35
De Castro, Calogero 1n1, 16

Deledda, Grazia 13, 47n59, 50n69
Di Giacomo, Salvatore 56n97
"Di guardia" ("Watch and Ward") 15, 29n1, 31n8, 41n37, 61
Di San Secondo, Rosso 46n54
Dialect vii, 2, 8, 8, 9, 19, 20, 21, 24, 25, 30n6, 33n11, 38n24, 39n28, 41n38, 51n75, 77, 78
Don Filippino 42, 42n40
"Donna Mimma" 21, 42n42, 43n45,
Drawings ix, xiv, 2, 3, 5, 16, 18, 19, 46n54, 57n99, 58n100,
"Due letti a due" ("Two Double Beds") 8, 45n52

Elegie renane (*Rhenish Elegies*) 46n53, 56n96
"Erba del nostro orto" ("The Grass in Our Garden") 55n89
Erma Bifronte (*Two-faced Herm*) 46n56, 55n93, 56n97
Essays 1, 3, 8, 52, 78
"Fuoco alla paglia" ("Set Fire to the Straw") 41n36

Fasci Siciliani 45n51
Father Innocenzo 38
Ferri, Giustino Lorenzo 46n55
Fileno (Dr.) 47n58
Florence 4, 32, 38n24, 53n84, 54n85
Fornello 35
Forno 35, 35n14
Faguet, Émile 48n62
Frainet 35, 36
Frangoro (Dr.) 33
Frau, Ombretta ix, xin2, xivn4, 23n7, 61
French 8, 48n62, 50, 50n70, 56n95
Friedrich, Caspar David 12
"Fuga" ("Escape") 41n37
Fuori di chiave (*Out of Tune*) 47n57, 56n96

Galleana 35
Garibaldi, Giuseppe 55n92
Garida 9, 35n14
Generalessa 15, 31, 31n7, 31n8, 63n104
Geography 9, 11
German(y) 8, 46n53, 54n87, 56, 56n95, 77
Giaveno 9, 29n2, 33, 34n13
"Gioventù" ("Youth") 13, 15, 29n1, 30n5, 32n9, 33n11,
Girgenti 9, 77
Giusti, Giuseppe 47n57
Giustino Roncella nato Boggiòlo (*Giustino Roncella Born Boggiòlo*) 13, 14, 45n48, 46n55
Gore 29n1
Gracci, Ugo 50n71
Gragnani, Cristina 23n7
Gramsci, Antonio 22
Grattarola (Mr.) 15, 33
"Guardando una stampa" ("Looking at a Print") 21

Harvard 5, 7, 23, 64n107, 66n112
Houghton Library (Harvard) ix, xiv, 2, 5, 7, 61,
Humor viii, 4, 12, 19, 46n55, 47n57, 51, 59, 63n104, 79

I vecchi e i giovani (*The Old and the Young*) 45n51, 48n61

Il berretto a sonagli (*Cap and Bells*) 51n75, 78
"Il "no" di Anna" ("Lost and Found") 44n48
"Il dovere del medico" ("The Doctor's Duty") 21
Il fu Mattia Pascal (*The Late Mattia Pascal*) 4, 8, 46n56, 49, 50, 50n69, 50n70, 55, 55n91, 56n95, 77
"Il fumo" ("The Fumes") 20, 22, 38n24, 41n38
"Il guardaroba dell'eloquenza" ("The Wardrobe of Eloquence") 40n34
Il piacere dell'onestà (*The Pleasure of Honesty*) 37n22
"Il professor Terremoto" ("Professor Earthquake")52n77
"Il sonno del vecchio" ("The Old Man's Slumber") 14
Il turno (*The Turn*) 36n20
"Il tabernacolo" ("The Shrine") 40n33
"Il vitalizio" ("The Annuity") 20, 38n24, 56, 56n95
"Il lume dell'altra casa" ("The Light from the House Opposite") 50n71
Illustration 2, 6, 16, 54n37
"Illustratori, attori e traduttori" ("Illustrators, Actors, and Translators") 25
Imagination 11, 12, 14, 15, 17, 18, 79, 81
Indritto 9, 35, 35n14
Italy vii, 1, 1n1, 8, 29n1, 29n2, 35n15, 38n24, 38n27, 46n53, 46n56, 48n60, 51n75, 55n92, 63n105
"Jeri e oggi" ("Yesterday and Today") 37n22
Journal de Genève 50n70
Jugend 54, 54n87

"L'altro figlio" ("The Other Son") 41n36
"L'avemaria di Bobbio" ("Bobbio's Hail Mary") 40n33
"La balia" ("The Wet Nurse") 20, 39n29
"La buon'anima" ("The Dearly Departed") 53n83
"La casa del Granella" ("Granella's House") 40n32
L'esclusa (*The Outcast*) 1
L'umorismo (*On Humor*) 12, 19, 46n55, 47n57, 51, 51n76, 59,
L'uomo, la bestia e la virtù (*Man, Beast, and Virtue*)21, 43n45
La camminante (The Walker) 8, 46, 46n55
La Gazzetta del Popolo 46, 46n55
La giara (*The Jar*) 45n52, 49n65, 50n68
La morsa (The Vise) 8, 51n73
La preparazione 47, 47n58, 48, 48n60, 49, 49n63
La Riviera Ligure 7, 12, 36, 36n19, 37, 37n23, 47, 47n57, 53, 53n83, 55, 55n93, 66n11
La tribuna 46n56
Landscape vii, viii, 10, 18, 19, 37n23
La vita nuda (*The Naked Life*) 53n83, 54n86
Lazarus (*Lazzaro*) 67n114, 78

Le Courage Civique 48, 48n62
"La fedeltà del cane" ("Man's Best Friend") 56, 56n98
"La lega disciolta" ("The League Dissolved") 40n33, 44n36, 52n77
"La messa di quest'anno" ("This Year's Mass") 15
"La morta e la viva" ("The Living and the Dead") 52n77
"La morte addosso" ("Death Is Upon Him") 40n35
"La scelta" ("The Choice") 43n45
"La signora Speranza" ("Mrs. Hope") 51n74
"La tragedia d'un personaggio" ("Tragedy of a Character")47n58
"La veglia" ("The Vigil") 54n88
"Leonora Addio!" ("Farewell, Leonora!") 52n77
"Le maschere" ("The Masks") 52n77
"Le medaglie" ("The Medals") 14, 55n92
"L'eresia catara" ("The Cathar Heresy") 55n93
"Levata del sole" ("Sunrise") 54n87
"Leviamoci questo pensiero" ("Let's Get Rid of this Thought") 52n77
"L'imbecille" ("The Imbecile") 54n89
"Lo scaldino" ("The Footwarmer") 43n45
L'epilogo (The Epilogue) 51n73
Liolà (*Liolà*) 8, 51n75
Lo Vecchio Musti, Manlio xiv, 5, 6n4, 37n23
"Lontano" ("Far Away") 36, 36n20, 47n58, 53n84,
"Lo spirito maligno" ("Evil Spirit") 52n77
"Lo storno e l'angelo centuno" ("The Starling and the One Hundred and One Angel") 52n77
"L'uccello impagliato" ("The Stuffed Bird 51n74
"Lumie di Sicilia" ("Sicilian Limes") 54n85

"Ma non è una cosa seria" ("But It's Nothing Serious") 49n65, 51n74
Macerata 37, 37n22
Maestro 2, 7
Manuscript xiii, xiv, xivn3, 2, 5, 6, 37n23, 44n47, 50n69, 52n79, 53n81, 57n99, 59n101, 61, 78
Manzoni, Alessandro 20
Marquise 39
Marsili Antonetti, Renata 1n1
"Marsina stretta" ("The Tight Frock") 29n2
Martoglio, Nino 8, 46n55, 54n86
Marzocco 45, 45n52, 49, 49n64, 53, 53n85, 54, 54n85, 54n86, 54n89, 55, 56, 56n98
Mattonera 35
Monaci, Ernesto 46n54
Mondadori xiv, 5, 6, 6n4, 7, 23n7, 37n23, 44n47, 52, 52m79, 53n81, 57n99, 58n100, 61
"Mondo di carta: ("Paper World") 49n65
Monte Luzera 36
Montepulciano ix, 4, 6, 20, 21, 22, 25, 38, 38n24, 39n27, 39n28, 40n32,

41n36, 41n37, 41n38, 44n47,
Mount Amiata 38
Mount Cetuna 38
Musco, Angelo 8, 51n75
"Musica vecchia" ("Old Music") 52n78

Naccheri (Mrs.) 38
Natura e Arte 52, 52n78
Nature 10, 11, 12, 17, 24, 26, 44, 45n48, 46n53, 46n54, 55n94, 56n96, 61, 63n104, 66n113, 67n114, 79
"Nel segno" ("Into the Sketch") 54, 54n85, 54n86,
"Nenè e Ninì" ("Nenè and Ninì") 40n33
Nobel Prize 1, 26, 50n69, 79
"Non conclude" ("It Won't End") 49n63
Notebook vii, viii, ix, 1n1, 2, 2n3, 3, 4, 5, 6, 7, 8, 9, 10, 12, 13, 14, 15, 16, 18, 19, 23, 24, 26, 52n79, 54n85, 58n100, 59n101, 63n106,
Novaro, Mario 35n19
Nuova Antologia 5, 23n7, 36, 36n20, 46, 46n54, 53, 53n84, 54n87, 55, 55n90,

"O di uno o di nessuno" ("Either One or None") 55n91
Orvieto, Adolfo 53n85

"Pallino e Mimì" ("Pallino and Mimì") 20, 39n27, 41n36
Pascoli, Giovanni 37n21, 55n91, 56n96, 56n97
Pasqua di Gea (*Easter of Gea*) 56n96
Paulo, Post (Dr.) 47n58
"Paura d'essere felice" ("Fear of Being Happy") 41n36
"Pena di vivere così" ("Such Is Life") 41n37
Pensaci Giacomino! (*Think it Over, Giacomino!*) 8, 49n65, 51n75, 78
Perugia 38n27
Pian del Viermo 35
Piedmont viii, 1, 30n6, 32, 33, 35n15, 42n42,
Piperino, Ugo 51n75
Pirandello, Fausto 6
Pirandello, Lina 1, 1n2, 16
Pirandello, Stefano xiii, xivn3, 1n1, 13, 37n22
Play 2, 4, 8, 13, 17, 22, 24, 30n3, 44n48, 45n51, 50n68, 51n73, 51n74, 51n75, 53n83, 54n88, 67n114, 78
Playwright vii, 1n1, 4, 8, 16, 21, 22, 23, 24, 38n24, 46n55, 59n101, 77, 78, 79
Po River 29n2
Portulano, Maria Antonietta 1, 77
Prever 13, 30, 30n5, 32n10
Prezzolini, Giuseppe 38n26
"Prima notte" ("Wedding Night") 54n85
Protonotari, Francesco 53n84

"Quando ero matto" ("When I Was Crazy")10, 37n20
"Quando si comprende" ("War") 37n22

Rassegna Contemporanea 48, 48n61, 49
Reda, Romualdo 15
Regina 56, 56n97
Revue politique et littéraire 48n62

"Rimedio: la geografia" ("Remedy: Geography") 11
Reviews 3, 8, 22, 52n78, 53n84
Righelli, Gennaro 51n75
Rio Fronteglio 35, 35n15
Rivista Popolare 45, 45n51
Roccia 25, 44, 44n46
Roccia Corba 36
Rocciavré 9
Rolando 36
Roma letteraria 46n53
Romantic 11, 12, 17, 46n53
Rome vii, 1, 1n1, 1n2, 10, 15, 16, 16n5, 37n21, 46n55, 51n75, 59n101, 77, 78
Ruadamonte 35
Rubinett 36
Rufinera 35

Sangone 9, 29, 29n2, 34n13, 35, 35n14, 35n15, 36n17, 64, 65n108, 66, 66n109,
Sangonetto 9, 35, 35n14
Santa Maria del Pino 16n6
Sarteano Castle 38, 38n26
Savoja 36
Sei personaggi in cerca d'autore (*Six Characters in Search of an Author*) 30n3, 78
Selvaggio 35
Sicily 77, 1n1, 10, 22, 36n20, 40n32, 41n38, 45n51
Siena 4, 38n24, 38n27
Silvia (Roncella) 13, 14, 36n17, 37n23, 45n48, 47n59, 55n94
Sipario 5
Soriano del Cimino 23, 46n54
Spingardi (Mrs.) 33
"Spunta un giorno" ("A New Day Rising") 20, 39n30
Stasera si recita a soggetto (Tonight We Improvise)30n3, 78
"Sua Maestà" ("Her Majesty") 40n32, 54n89
Sul Bosforo d'Italia (*On the Italian Bosphorus*) 8, 45n53
Sulphur Mines 22, 36n20, 41n38, 44n46
Suo marito (*Her Husband*) 13, 30n4, 32n10, 33, 36n17, 37n23, 45n48, 47n59, 50n69, 55n94

Taccuino di Bonn xiii, 23, 23n7
Taccuino di Harvard 23, 23n7, 66n112
Taccuino segreto 23, 23n7
Teatro dei Filodrammatici 17
Teatro Siciliano? (*Sicilian Theater?)* 8, 45n51
Terni 38n27
Theater 5, 8, 45n50, 45n51, 46n55, 67n114, 78, 81
The Mountain Giants (*I giganti della montagna*) 67n114, 78
The New Colony (*La nuova colonia*) 67n114
Titans 67
Tofano, Sergio 51n75
Tonache di Montelusa (*Cassocks of Montelusa*) 49n64
Tra castagni e olivi (*Among Chestnut and Olive Trees*) 8
"Tra due ombre" ("Between Two Shadows") 41n37
Trasimeno (Lake) 38, 38n27
Treves 46, 46n56, 48n61, 49, 49n67, 50n69, 50n70, 53n83

Turin xiv, 1, 29n2, 36n18
Tuscany 7, 38n26, 38n27

Uja 36
Umbria 38n27
"Una voce" ("A Voice")
56n97
Uno, nessuno e centomila
(One, None, and a
Hundred Thousand)49n63

Val Chisone 9, 29n2
Val di Susa 9, 29n2, 34n13
Valgioje 33
Valsusa 29, 33
Velia (Aunt) 15, 30n5, 32n9,
32n10, 33n12,
Verga, Giovanni 21, 46n56,
78
Verismo 8, 21, 46n53, 78
Vernacular vii, 2, 8, 21, 22,
24, 38n24, 38n25, 50n34
Villareto 35
Viretta 36
Visual 2, 3, 5, 6, 11, 15, 16,
18, 19, 81
"Va bene" ("It's fine") 41n36
"Visto che non piove" ("Since
It's Not Raining") 40n34
"Volare" ("Flying") 40n34

Waldesians 17n6
World War I 37n22, 54n85

Zampogna (*Bagpipes*) 37,
37n21, 54n85, 56n96, 77
Zane 29, 29n1, 65
Zappulla Muscarà, Sarah
36n19, 54n86
Zighi 30n6, 65

About the Author

Luigi Pirandello was born in 1867 in Girgenti (now Agrigento) in Sicily. He became an internationally renowned playwright, novelist, essayist, and short-story writer. The son of a sulfur merchant, Pirandello entered the University of Rome in 1887 and later transferred to Bonn where he completed his doctoral studies and wrote a thesis on his native Sicilian dialect. His experiences in Germany frequently returned in his future poetic, fictional, and theoretical works.

In 1894, Pirandello agreed to an arranged marriage to Antonietta Portulano, with whom he had three children and settled in Rome where he began teaching at a local women's college until 1923. In 1903, the loss of his father's fortune brought financial worries and contributed to his wife's mental illness, which degenerated until her institutionalization in 1919. Antonietta's illness had a profound effect on Pirandello's writing, leading him to explore what became the staple tropes of his poetics: madness, illusion, and isolation.

Although Pirandello first channeled his creativity into verse, as attested by the seminal collections *Troubled Joy* (1887), *Easter in Gea* (1891), *Rhenish Elegies* (1895), *Bagpipes* (1901), and *Offkey* (1912), his attention turned to naturalistic fiction under the influence of Sicilian novelist Luigi Capuana. Pirandello's first novel *The Outcast* (1893) was followed by his first widely-acclaimed book *The Late Mattia Pascal* (1904), *The Old and The* Young (1913) and *One, None, and a Hundred Thousand* (1925–26).

Pirandello's passion for storytelling was also manifested through the short story, a mode to which he showed an extraordinary, long-lasting devotion. His body of work includes numerous pieces of short fiction written from the time he was a teenager until a few days before his death in 1936. His intention was to offer his readers 365 stories—a story for every day of the year—through an ambitious collection of twenty-four volumes, each containing fifteen stories. Posthumously, the 234 tales he had composed were collected into the two-volume *Stories for a Year,* which included the tales initially left out from the collection, some new manuscripts, and numerous variants of previous texts.

It was only in 1910 that Pirandello engaged with theatre. Enthralled by the medium's expressive potential, he became a prolific playwright, writing over 40 plays throughout his career. His theatrical production is generally divided into four phases influenced by different themes and styles: the so-called *Verista* theater (1910-1916), which is deeply linked to regional and dialectal leitmotifs inspired by Sicilian culture and authors—namely Giovanni Verga, (*Sicilian Limes* [1910], *Think it Over, Giacomino!* [1916], *Liolà* [1916], and *Cap and Bells* [1917]); the 'grotesque' and relativist phase (1916-1920), which was marked by comic tragedies (or tragic comedies) and juxtaposed the contrasting dyad of life and form (*Right You Are* (*If You Think You Are*) [1917], *The Pleasure of Honesty* [1917], and *The Rules of the Game* [1918]); the phase of the "theater within the theater," which launched Pirandello's first notable critical successes *Six Characters in Search of an Author, Each in His Own Way* (1924), and *Tonight We Improvise* (1930); and a fourth "mythical" phase (1928-1936), marked by the authorial predilection to explore a fantastic dimension beyond time and reality (*The New Colony* [1928], *Lazarus* [1929], and *The Giants of the Mountain* [1930]).

Between 1922 and 1924, Pirandello became a major public figure in the artistic and political scene. In 1925, with the support of Mussolini, he founded his own *Art Theatre* in Rome, an unfortunate artistic enterprise that came to an end in 1928 due to financial constraints while a disillusioned Pirandello went into voluntary exile in Berlin (1928-30) and Paris (1930).

Pirandello was a complex artist, whose brilliant storytelling and dramatic originality went hand-in-hand with his critical activity. His seminal essays, *Art and Consciousness*

Today (1889), *On Humor* (1908), and *Art and Science* (1908), offer an illuminating analysis of the conflicted relationship between art and life and the role the artist's imagination plays in it. Pirandello's innovative examination of the paradoxical nature of reality had a great impact on later playwrights, and he was awarded the Nobel Prize in Literature in 1934 "for his bold and ingenious revival of dramatic and scenic art."

About the Editor

Lisa Sarti is Associate Professor of Italian at BMCC of The City University of New York in Manhattan. Her main field of research is fin-de-siècle visual culture, early cinematography, and the interplay of literature and the performing arts. She has published studies on Arrigo Boito, Melodrama, Annie Vivanti and the Female artists of the *Cafè Chantant*, American musical theater, and Pirandello's storytelling and theatre, as well the cinematic adaptation of his short stories. She co-edited (with Michael Subialka) the volume *Pirandello's Visual Philosophy: Imagination and Thought Across Media* (Fairleigh Dickinson UP, 2017) and she co-authored (with Carlo Di Lieto and Michael Subialka) the book *Scrittura d'immagini: Pirandello e la visualità tra letteratura, filosofia e psicanalisi* (Rubbettino 2021). Professor Sarti is the co-editor of *PSA-The Journal of the Pirandello Society of America* and of *Stories for a Year*, a digital humanities project aiming at translating and publishing the complete short stories of Luigi Pirandello.

ROBERT VISCUSI
–1941-2020–

Robert Viscusi was fundamental to the development of Bordighera Press; to its journal *VIA*: *Voices in Italian Americana*, and to the book series *VIA* FOLIOS.

One of his many ground-breaking articles, "Breaking the Silence: Strategic Imperatives for Italian American Culture," opened *VIA*'s inaugural issue. In like fashion, his keenly satiric, genial long poem, "An Oration upon the Most Recent Death of Christopher Columbus," was the stimulus for the founding our first book series, *VIA* FOLIOS.

In later years we also published his epic poem, *Ellis Island*, a collection of sonnets whose "Star Review" from *Publishers Weekly* closed as follows: "[T]he sonnets are far from uniform, at times manifesting as short stories, at other times as short bursts of philosophical inquiry or bursts of pure song. This is a new delicacy for aficionados of creative poetry and an anthem of sorts for those who – however far removed from immigration – occasionally feel displaced from home."

ROBERT VISCUSI ESSAY SERIES

Named in honor of the work of Robert Viscusi, this referred series is dedicated to the long essay. It intends to publish studies that are longer than the traditional journal-length essay and yet shorter than the traditional book-length manuscript. All books are peer-reviewed.

Linda L. Carroll. *Thomas Jefferson's Italian and Italian-Related Books in the History of Universal Personal Rights. An Overview.* Volume 1.

Luisa Del Giudice, ed. *Triangulations within the Italy-Canada-United States.* Volume 2.

Alfred R. Crudale. *The Voices of Italy: Italian Language Newspapers and Radio Programs in Rhode Island.* Volume 3.

Pasquale Stiso's "True Story" and Other Works: A Critical Introduction and Bilingual Edition. Laura E. Ruberto and Pasquale Verdicchio, eds. Volume 4.

Luigi Pirandello. *The Coazze Notebook.* Translation and Introduction by Lisa Sarti. Volume 5.